COMANCHES, CAPTIVES, AND GERMANS

COMANCHES CAPTIVES AND GERMANS

Wilhelm Friedrich's Drawings from the Texas Frontier

DANIEL J.
GELO

C.B. "HOPPY"
HOPKINS

CHRISTOPHER J.
WICKHAM

BRYDEN E.
MOON JR.

The Texas Center
Schreiner University · Kerrville, TX
325-660-1752 · www.mcwhiney.org

Cataloging-in-Publication Data

Names: Gelo, Daniel J., C. B. "Hoppy" Hopkins, Christopher J. Wickham, and Bryden E. Moon Jr., authors.
Title: Comanches, captives, and Germans: Wilhelm Friedrich's drawings from the Texas frontier / Daniel J. Gelo, C. B. "Hoppy" Hopkins, Christopher J. Wickham, and Bryden E. Moon Jr.
Description: First edition. | Kerrville, TX: State House Press, 2022. | Includes bibliographical references, illustrations, and index.
Identifiers: ISBN 9781649670137 (soft cover); ISBN 9781649670151 (e-book)
Subjects: LCSH: Comanche Indians – Texas – 19th century – Pictorial works. | Germans – Texas – History – 19th century. | Friedrich, Wilhelm, 1823—1868.
Classification: LCC E99.C85 (print) | DCC 976.4

First edition 2022

Cover and page design by Allen Griffith of Eye 4 Design.

Distributed by Texas A&M University Press Consortium
800-826-8911
www.tamupress.com

In memory of Timothy Koock 1944-2022

CONTENTS

AUTHORS AND ACKNOWLEDGEMENTS

Daniel J. Gelo is Dean and Professor of Anthropology Emeritus at the University of Texas at San Antonio. C.B. "Hoppy" Hopkins is an independent researcher in Fredericksburg, Texas. Christopher J. Wickham is Professor of German Emeritus at the University of Texas at San Antonio. Bryden E. Moon Jr. is an independent researcher in Boerne, Texas.

This book is the product of an exemplary dialogic research approach. The four primary authors recognize Timothy Koock, who first saw the potential for the project and introduced the authors to the drawing owners. Owners Robert Phelps and Brent Evans also saw the significance of the works, facilitated the research, and contributed energetically to the interpretations herein. Clara Snyder, Digital Archivist at the National Museum of the Pacific War, kindly produced scans of the Phelps drawings which greatly aided our examination. We also wish to thank: Douglas Boyd of Prewitt and Associates; Frau Dr. Annegret Holtmann-Mares of the Technical University of Darmstadt; Beverly Wigley of the Sophienberg Museum and Archives in New Braunfels, TX; Amy Rushing, Assistant Dean for Special Collections, and Vanessa F. Ramos and the interlibrary loan staff, John Peace Library, University of Texas at San Antonio; Caren Creech, Patrick Heath Public Library, Boerne, TX; Evelyn Weinheimer, Pioneer Museum, Fredericksburg, TX; and Glenn Hadeler.

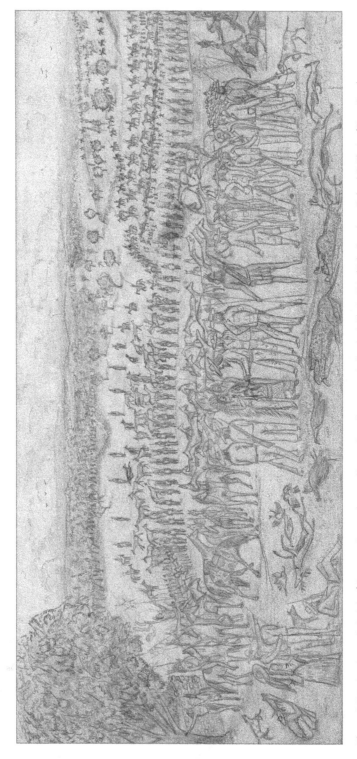

Figure 1. Drawing 1, pencil sketch of German–Comanche meeting and captive presentation by Wilhelm Friedrich. Courtesy Robert B. Phelps/Clara Snyder.

THE DISCOVERY

Three drawings of historical significance recently came to the attention of a small circle of researchers studying the relationship between the German settlers and Comanche Indians on the Texas frontier. The three drawings are closely related, and together they tell a story of the earliest days of German-Comanche interaction in 1847 in some remarkable detail. Drawing 1 (D1) is a 7 5/8" by 15 3/4" pencil sketch of a large meeting of Indians and white men with several details of their interaction and surroundings (Figure 1). This drawing has never been published before. Drawing 2 (D2), in the possession of a different owner, is a pen-and-ink rendering of the same scene shown in D1, by the same artist, measuring 9 1/2" by 17 1/2" (Figure 2). This version has been reproduced in Evans (2010, 12–13). We have numbered these two pieces consecutively since they require comparison. Drawing 3 (D3), in pencil by the same artist again, is a different scene: a train of ox-drawn wagons proceeding on a trail, with mounted Indians watching from above in the foreground, measuring 11 1/4" by 14 5/8" (Figure 3). Drawing 3 has been the companion of D1, is in the possession of the same owner, and has also not been published before.

2

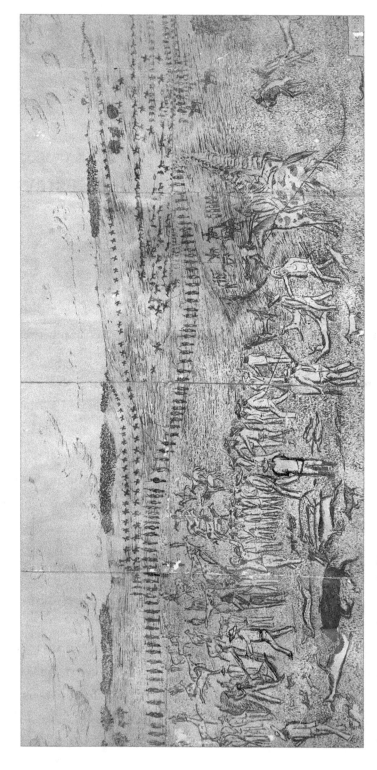

Figure 2 Drawing 2, pen and ink sketch of German–Comanche meeting and captive presentation by Wilhelm Friedrich. Courtesy Brent Evans.

Figure 3. Drawing 3, pencil sketch of wagon train by Wilhelm Friedrich.
Courtesy Robert B. Phelps/Clara Snyder.

Drawings 1 and 3 were inherited by Robert Phelps of Fredericksburg, Texas, from the estate of his maternal aunt Sally Duncan and her husband, Baker Duncan, Jr., in January 2020 (Phelps 2021). Both sketches have typewritten descriptions clipped from a sale catalog glued to their backing, to which were added handwritten dates and comments. D1 is given a date of 1849, and D3 is dated to 1848. The comments on both indicate that they had been bought by Martha Chancellor from the "Herff Estate" in the 1930s. Martha Violet Wood Chancellor (1897–1988) was a San Antonio antiques dealer specializing in early Texas and particularly early San Antonio. According to Mr. Phelps's cousin Baker Duncan, III, Duncan father and son made regular buying

Figure 4. Herff Home. Boerne. Courtesy Brent Evans.

visits to "Ms. Martha's" and the items were purchased on one of these occasions, sometime during the 1980s. It was the cousin's opinion that if any other similar items had been for sale at the time, they would have bought those too. Mr. Phelps was long intrigued by his uncle's sketches and requested them as a legacy. "Herff estate" refers to early German settler and noted physician Ferdinand Herff and his family, whose historical role will be explained below.

Drawing 2 is also directly associated with the Herff family (Evans 2021). Its ownership is traceable to Charles A. Herff (1855–1944), third son of Ferdinand Herff.[1] Charles inherited the Herff Farm in Boerne, Texas, and sold it out of the family in 1935 owing to financial difficulties (the estate sale at which Martha Chancellor bought D1 and D3 probably resulted from this house sale). When Charles was elderly and living in a care home the sketch passed to his sister-in-law Florence

Herff. Florence gave it to her daughter Juanita Herff Chipman, who in turn passed it to her son-in-law Brent Evans, husband of Carolyn Chipman Evans. The Evanses are co-founders of the Cibolo Center for Conservation in Boerne, Texas, and they have placed D2 on display in the beautifully preserved Herff farmhouse (Figure 4), which is on the center property, along with a finely wrought drawing of the Herff family tree.

COMANCHES, CAPTIVES, AND GERMANS

CHAPTER ONE
ᴛHE HISTORY

The setting for the drawings and the people associated with them is the German colonization of Central Texas during the 1840s and early 1850s (e.g., Gelo and Wickham 2018, 8–32). German immigrants populated the region under a colonization program organized by a society of German nobles with Prince Carl of Solms-Braunfels as commissioner general and known as the Adelsverein. Though the project was fraught with poor planning, severe underfinancing, financial mismanagement, physical hardship, and death, German settlers established stable communities at New Braunfels (1845) and Fredericksburg (1846). From the latter town, they were poised to move north across the Llano River into a 3.9-million-acre tract where the society had purchased settlement rights for them, known as the Fisher-Miller Grant. This enormous territory was yet unoccupied by whites and home to potentially hostile Native people belonging to several tribal groups, most notably Comanches.

Integral to the success of those seeking to occupy the Fisher-Miller Grant was a peace accord with the local Comanche bands belonging to the southern or Penateka ("Honey Eaters" in Comanche) division, pursued and consummated by Prince Carl's successor as commissioner general, John O. Meusebach. The nomadic Penateka bands favored the region between the Llano and Colorado Rivers, corresponding to the Fisher-Miller Grant, for its game, pecans, and winter horse pasturage, and maintained regular camp sites therein (Gelo and Wickham 2018, 1–8, 120–24). Meusebach and party explored the area in February–March 1847 and met with Penateka headmen Ketumsee, Buffalo Hump, Old Owl, and Santa Anna. They negotiated a pact ratified two months later in Fredericksburg. In dealing with the Comanches, the Germans were more tolerant than contemporary Anglo settlers, addressing the Indians as equals, inviting them to visit the German settlements regularly, and even acknowledging the eventual probability of language sharing and ethnic intermarriage.[1] The Meusebach accord has gained legendary status as a treaty never broken, and while there was trouble between Germans and Indians in the years that followed, none clearly involved the Penateka signatories, and the agreement allowed the Germans a foothold in the trans-Llano region.

Among the immigrants was a distinct group formed in Germany by young university men planning to establish their own utopian colony of freethinkers. Originating in and around the Hessian city of Darmstadt, they migrated to Texas together in the summer of 1847 under the leadership of Dr. Ferdinand Herff and Hermann Spiess, and became known as the Darmstadt Forty (or Gesellschaft der Vierziger, Darmstädter, Darmstaedter in German; "Darmstadter[s]," "The Forty," "Fortiers" in English). After a staging period, in the fall of 1847 the Forty migrated by ox wagon train across the Llano, the first settlers to do so, and selected a site on the north side of the river a mile or so downriver from present Castell, Texas. They named their commune Bettina in honor of the Italo-German writer, artist, and activist Bettina von Arnim. Four other tenuous settlements arose nearby, of which only Castell remains today, albeit relocated to the south side of the river. Bettina was also among the first of the German communities in Texas and the Midwest that became known as Latin settlements because their settlers were classically educated and sought to perpetuate a sophisticated culture in their new communities. The Forty raised 200 bushels of corn their first season, but conflict arose over work responsibilities, and Bettina fell apart within a year (Reinhardt 1899; Heinemann 1994, 324–333). The Fortiers returned to Germany or dispersed into other frontier communities. One of these men was the artist responsible for the drawings under consideration.

OUR FRIEND

WM. FRIEDRICH

DIED

DEC. 23, 1868

CHAPTER TWO
ℭHE ᴀRTIST

The identity of the artist or artists was not readily apparent, but a box drawn in the lower right corner of D2 contains a name and year neatly penned in a Fraktur calligraphic hand that, despite some flaking of the paper, read "Friedrich" and "1847" or "1849." Since the box is integral to the composition, we may assume that the artist was the person who filled it in with name and date. The name "Friedrich" appears again in pencil script in the lower right corner of D3. Drawing 1 lacks a name, but its similarity to D2 in subject matter and D3 in style, and the fact that it has been a companion piece to D3 through time, allows attribution to the same artist. On the assumptions that Friedrich was the artist's name and that he or she followed common practice and signed a surname rather than a given name, a search was made through published listings of the early German settlers around Fredericksburg, Texas; only once did the surname appear and the identity of Wilhelm Friedrich was disclosed. Family lore passed down to the owners of D2 confirmed Wilhelm Friedrich as the author of that work. This name is not among the most prominent ones in the annals of German settlement; thus far Friedrich has not been the subject of a complete biography, but his life course can be assembled from various references, much as was done recently for another important early German settler in Texas, Emil Kriewitz (1822–1902) (Gelo and Wickham 2018, 69–81). The evidence is clear that Wilhelm Friedrich was a member of the Darmstadt Forty and a close associate of Ferdinand Herff.[1]

Friedrich was born in 1823 in an unverified location in Germany, probably Griedel, the home town noted when he entered school and when he joined the Forty. Griedel is a district of the town of Butzbach in the Wetterau region of Hesse; the town lies forty-five miles north of Darmstadt, in territory once within the principality of Solms-Braunfels. Like several of the Forty, Friedrich attended the Höhere Gewerbeschule zu Darmstadt (Darmstadt Vocational School), forerunner of today's Technical University of Darmstadt. We are fortunate to have two of his handwritten grade reports from this school from the period 1840–1843 (ULB 1836–1841, 229; ULB 1841–1843, 43; translated by Wickham).[2] These records indicate that Friedrich entered the Darmstadt School at age eighteen, after attending the Realschule (public secondary school) in Giessen. His father's occupation is noted once as (what appears to read) bursary officer, and another time as a clergyman. Friedrich's own "occupation" (major) is listed as "Cameralist"; cameralism was a German social science focusing on the bureaucratic management of the nation state, containing prototypic elements of economics, statistics, public policy, and planning, and with the aim of producing enlightened administrators. This disciplinary focus is not obvious in Friedrich's curriculum, however, which consisted of an array of courses in history, languages, math, science, and drafting, pointing more toward a technical career.

The handwritten comments of Friedrich's various teachers, though not always clearly decipherable, are at times prophetic. He was weak in math and in languages, particularly English, but satisfactory in most other subjects, perhaps more able and interested in the hard sciences than the others. Despite the temperate appraisals of his academic results, the word "diligent" is frequently used to describe his efforts, and it seems his teachers at least admired his spirit. The one area where Friedrich was deemed exceptional was drawing, be it topographical, geometric, machine, or architectural. "Promises to become good" wrote Professor K. in March 1841; "Is developing very well in topographical drawing" wrote K. later; "Draws very well and with great earnestness" wrote another. The extant records do not confirm that Friedrich completed his course of study or graduated from the Darmstadt school, but we may assume he did, because the Forty's settlement proposal to the Adelsverein limited membership to those who had passed their exams and established themselves in their occupations (Heinemann 1994, 289).

At school, Friedrich was a member of the Corps Starkenburgia fraternity, whose motto is "loyalty and brotherly love." In this environment he heard the stirrings to form an emigrant party of young idealists, some of them delivered by Prince Carl of Solms-Braunfels himself. When questions arose about the financial viability of further Adelsverein projects, Friedrich was one of three Forty members to sign a declaration on behalf of the group, published in *Der deutsche Auswanderer* newspaper, professing their zeal for establishing a truly German community in Texas (Friedrich, Schenck, and Schleicher 1847).[3] Friedrich would have been about twenty-four years of age when he emigrated, typical of the recent graduates who, with some farmers, tradesmen, and professionals, a few of them older, constituted the Darmstadters.

Friedrich appears by first and last name, or last name only, on all of the rosters of the Forty immigrants. He also appears in the ship's manifest of the *St. Pauli*, the vessel that Forty recruits sailed on from Hamburg to Galveston. In fact, he is listed there twice, as two people, Wilhelm Fried(e)rich and Wilhelm Frederick; immigrants were not infrequently recorded by their correct name upon departure, and another Anglicized version when they disembarked. The party convened in Hamburg in February 1847. The *St. Pauli* set sail in April and arrived in Galveston on July 4.

With significant delays, the party made its way from Galveston to Indianola, then to New Braunfels. In New Braunfels they witnessed the visit of a Penateka delegation under Santa Anna which had come to claim gifts promised in the Meusebach Treaty, seeing for the first time their future neighbors (Heinemann 1994, 323–24). From New Braunfels they traveled through Fredericksburg to the site of their colony on the Llano River, arriving in late September. In the online data for Galveston immigration, Friedrich's destination is recorded as Mason County. This detail, however, is an anachronism introduced by a compiler, because in 1847 the area that would become Mason County was within Gillespie County, itself only recently separated from Bexar County; Mason County was established only in 1858 (Rhoads 2010).

Friedrich did arrive at Bettina, presumably with the founders' wagon train in September, though he is not mentioned in accounts of that journey and could have gotten there by other means. While on his way he signed an affidavit in Comal County on September 7, 1847, testifying to his origin and status as a single male over seventeen years of age, which made him eligible for an Adelsverein land grant of 320 acres (Affidavit). He also probably worked on the Darmstadt Farm, a settlement the eager Forty started near New Braunfels while waiting there for some members to regain their health prior to venturing beyond the Llano.[4] By the following summer Friedrich secured a certificate and survey of property in the Fisher-Miller grant, thirteen miles northwest of present Llano, Texas (Field Notes). It appears that he did not occupy this land immediately, if ever, but instead managed its acquisition while living as a member of the Bettina commune. His presence at Bettina is confirmed in Herff's recollections of the colony, wherein Herff named Friedrich among the hardworking and honest colonists who stood apart from those who soon became jaded with the enterprise and maneuvered to drop out without financial loss (Morgenthaler 2007, 101). An alternate reading of this assessment is that Friedrich was not among those several settlers who quickly found Herff and Spiess's leadership too communistic or dictatorial (see Reichstein 2001, 51–59). However it is interpreted, Friedrich's loyalty would continue to shape his life course. It may be assumed that he stayed at the commune for most of its existence, though there is no full account of his time there.

A roster of the Forty members published in the newspaper on the eve of their departure from Germany lists Friedrich's profession with a title probably best translated as "public administrator" ("Namensverzeichniß der Darmstädter Texasauswanderer" 1847, translated by Wickham). This title is in keeping with his cameralist student status as reflected in the records of the Höhere Gewerbeschule and his Starkenburgia fraternity listing. His cameralist profession is specified in one place, the list of Fortiers reconstructed by the early historian of the German pioneers Adolph Paul Weber (Weber 1894, part 1, page 26). On most of the lists of Fortiers, however, Friedrich is listed as "lawyer," one of seven members with this occupation, among others listed as physician (including Herff), engineer, architect, blacksmith, carpenter, farmer, forester, theology student, butcher, and so on. The "lawyer" designation for Friedrich probably started as an oversimplification of his German public administration title, for there is no evidence that he studied toward or earned a law degree.[5] In any event, only some of the colonists could reasonably expect to pursue their designated occupations in the early days of the Bettina settlement. The notable example was Herff, who pledged to minister to the others as physician in the written settlement agreement the Darmstadters made with the Adelsverein (Spiess Papers, 68). There was certainly no need for five foresters on the Llano River, even though the Germans were pleasantly surprised by the woods lining a river named for its relatively treeless aspect. All the colonists were chopping what wood they could find, and plowing too, at least until many decided that they were above such work and the colony fell apart. So while there may have been naïve expectations of staffing a complete society in the new settlement, the listed occupations mainly indicate the professions that the settlers were training for or starting in when recruited, and there is no reason to believe that Friedrich functioned as an attorney in Bettina. Most of the Forty did go on with their vocations after Bettina dissolved (Hertzberg and Schenck 1988, 148), but there is no evidence Friedrich ever practiced law (or public administration), and at most he relied on any training he might have obtained in these subjects to guide his business ventures.

The fortitude that Herff praised was in evidence as Friedrich continued to build a life for himself once the experiment on the Llano failed. After Bettina he is found in New Braunfels, possibly working on the Darmstadt Farm during its closing days, for a William Frederick, "labourer," born in 1822 in Germany, is counted in that town in the U.S. census of September 1850. (In subsequent records, Friedrich often appears as "William," with various surname spellings. He entered "William" himself on certain documents.) On May 15 of that year, Friedrich bought 400 acres from John James at a dollar per acre west of today's downtown Boerne, on present Johns Road between Main Street and IH-10 (Morgenthaler 2007, 108–110; 2014, 28–30; Evans 2010, 9). This well-watered property straddled the Camino San Saba (Camino Viejo, San Saba Road), an ancient Indian and Spanish pathway that, together with the roughly parallel Pinta Trail to the east, connected San Antonio with Fredericksburg and points beyond. Here Friedrich would be joined by a small group of ex-Fortiers and other Germans, who with him built a compound for a new Latin settlement that predated the establishment of the town of Boerne (Moon 2020).[6] Another Bettina expatriate, Christian Hesse, purchased a large adjacent plot.

In less than a year, however, Friedrich sold the commune property to another member, Adam Vogt, for four times what he paid for it, and bought forty-four acres, also from John James, less than a mile southeast of the new commune and just touching on the Camino San Saba, to set up his own farmstead. This parcel, Lot 32, lay in the southwest corner of a plot assembled by James and fellow speculator Gustav Theissen as the Boerne townsite. The deed for this transaction, which records Friedrich as a resident of Fredericksburg, bears the postscript: "Signed sealed and delivered in presence of Dr. F. Herff." Thus Friedrich, with Herff's endorsement, was one of four original lot owners in the new town. The earliest town plat, dated 1852, shows Friedrich's property lying along the bend of a creek that joins Cibolo Creek, all just west of the present Main Street crossing (Evans 2010, 18; Morgenthaler 2014, 11). The tributary was originally known as Friedrich Creek, but fairly soon the name started to be Anglicized as Frederick Creek, and it appears this way on modern maps (Morgenthaler 2007, 110; 2014, 30).[7] Within a few years the new commune folded. While some of its other subscribers moved onto nearby properties as Friedrich had done, most dispersed for other places. One source states that Friedrich moved to San Antonio during this period (Weber 1894, part 2, page 8). Over time Friedrich sold off six of the original acres in Lot 32, but augmented the parcel with an adjoining twenty-four acres to the north. These lands would be sold in 1886 by Friedrich's heirs, and the following year, with the arrival of the San Antonio and Aransas Pass Railroad in Boerne, his former acreage was marketed to San Antonians as part of "Irons' and Graham's Addition" in "the great health resort of Boerne" (Evans 2010, 19; Anderson 2019). Such ambitious development plans were never realized, but the town had been thrust into a new era, and new streets and housing on the old Friedrich property gave rise to a mixed neighborhood of African Americans, Mexicans, English, Irish, and Germans that became known as "The Flats" (Benedict 2021).

Between 1854 and 1861 Friedrich made his living as a surveyor. He was employed as Deputy Surveyor with the Bexar Land District, first under fellow ex-Fortier Gustav Schleicher, and then under François Giraud, a San Antonian who in addition to serving as chief county surveyor was an architect and associate of Ferdinand Herff. His attending chain carriers over time included former Bettina associates and well-known early Kendall County residents (there was good money to be made carrying chains [Lindheimer 1848, column 779]). Files in the Texas General Land Office contain some fifty-seven surveys that Friedrich completed in what would become Kendall County. As predicted by his teachers in Germany, Friedrich's draftsmanship was always more than a notch above the usual. An October 1860 survey he produced of some property in present northwest San Antonio is characteristically superb, preserving heretofore unknown detail of the linkage between the Camino Real and the Pinta Trail, routes which the German pioneers used to reach Fredericksburg (Texas General Land Office, Abstract 482, Survey 391; Figure 5). Two more of his survey drawings show two otherwise unrecorded trails that the Germans blazed to link Boerne with Comfort and Sisterdale (Abstract 386, Survey 23½; Abstract 184, Survey 6½). And though he earned only fair marks for English in school, and it was said that none of the men at Bettina were fluent in the language, Friedrich evidently mastered at least the written form in his early post-commune years, for his survey documents contain exemplary grammar, word choice, and spelling. Survey work opened additional business opportunities for Friedrich, and he became very active in speculating on lands throughout the Fisher-Miller Grant. He appears as patentee on several grants made to former Fortiers and other German settlers, sometimes in partnership with Giraud (Land Grant Files). When homesteaders along the Guadalupe River and Cibolo Creek petitioned the Texas Legislature to form a new county with Boerne as its seat in 1855 and again in 1859, Friedrich signed his name with a distinctive Hancockian flourish (Petition 1855, 1859). Herff joined him in signing the 1859 appeal.

Ferdinand Herff also began buying property around Boerne. Like some other Fortiers, Herff had returned to Germany as the Llano commune dissolved. In Darmstadt he married, published a treatise advising future emigrants based on the hard lessons of Bettina (Herff

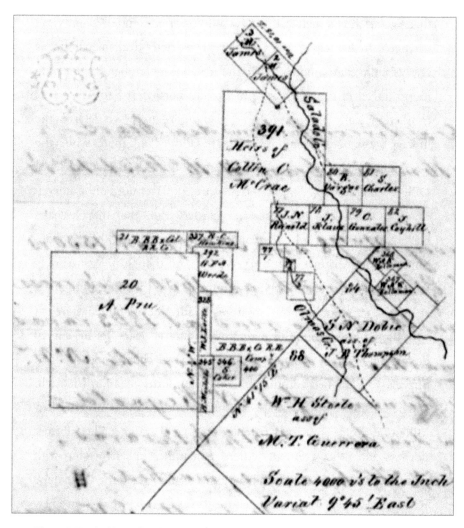

Figure 5. Friedrich's plat for Abstract 482, Survey 391, dated October 10, 1860, showing convergence of Pinta Trail (long dotted line) and cut-off from Camino Real (short dotted line). The convergence place is on present southern Camp Bullis just north of Eisenhower Park, San Antonio. Courtesy of Bryden E. Moon Jr.

1978), and fulfilled his duty as a combat surgeon in the Hessian army. But his plan remained to live in Texas. He came back first to New Braunfels, and it was probably there that he and Wilhelm Friedrich reconnected. In April 1850 Herff moved to San Antonio, and went on there to establish a prosperous practice, achieve notable advances in medicine, and raise an illustrious family. No doubt the continuing presence of his old Fortier friends in Boerne attracted Herff to that area, and over time he amassed some ten thousand acres in the Hill Country (Morgenthaler 2007, 110). Some of his land was adjacent to Friedrich's creekside property and more was situated away from the town center. Herff acquired 640 acres directly south of the new commune site, then sold 346 acres of it to Friedrich in 1856 (Abstract 310, Survey 178; Morgenthaler 2014, 30). Eventually Herff built a stately home southeast of downtown Boerne as a country retreat. During the period of real estate fervor in the 1850s Friedrich not only renewed his friendship with Herff, but was practically adopted by the Herffs as a family member. He officially lived in Mason County in 1859 according to one source (Reichstein 2001, 65). In February 1860, he was listed as a charter member of the board of trustees for the German-English School in San Antonio (McGuire 1976, 89, n. 103).

Friedrich was single when he immigrated, and he probably worried like other German newcomers about ever finding a suitable spouse on the frontier. On February 18, 1860, "William" Friedrich married Alice André, a woman of English birth, at St. Mary's Catholic Church in San Antonio. Like several of his colleagues, Friedrich wed a considerably younger woman; he was about 37, and she about 18. The U.S. census from June of that year shows that they resided in a boarding house in San Antonio's First Ward, and that the value of Friedrich's personal estate was a respectable $20,000, over $600,000 in 2021 dollars. They went on to have two daughters, Charlotte Mathilde, "Lotta," whose middle name was apparently given in honor of Ferdinand Herff's wife, and Alice Louise.

A charming glimpse of the man Friedrich had become is offered in a 1927 letter handed down by the descendants of Conrad Adam, another settler in the Boerne area: "Papa had a rich uncle in America, Wilhelm Friedrich . . . . This uncle persuaded Papa [Conrad Adam] to come to America. This uncle was a surveyor as it was called. It was said that he owned a great deal of land . . . he always was one of the foremost men in Kendall County and a very good friend of old Doctor Herff" (*sic*; Adam-Hurst 2012).

In 1861, with civil war approaching, Friedrich had the idea of setting up a gunpowder factory in San Antonio to supply the Confederacy.[8] For this new business, Friedrich drew on his knowledge of another main subject in his vocational school training: chemistry. He may also have figured on exploiting the copious deposits of bat guano available in caves along the Balcones Escarpment. He must have invested deeply from his personal wealth. His new concern prospered for a while, but declined as competing powder factories grew up around the south during the war, and then the conflict wound down. Now under serious financial strain, he moved in with the Herff family temporarily. Friedrich continued to run the plant after the war ended. It appears that the federal troops occupying San Antonio during Reconstruction decided not to close the factory, probably because they intended for San Antonio to continue as the major supply depot for westward expansion. Friedrich converted his operation to produce blasting powder for construction projects, and his future again looked promising.

But about December 20, 1868, Friedrich's factory was the scene of a massive explosion. All thirteen of his workers were killed instantly, and Friedrich suffered horrific burns over 80 per cent of his body. He lay in agony for three days under the constant care of an anguished Dr. Herff, before passing on December 23.[9] The Herffs saw to it that their dear friend was buried next to their son Baldwin, who had died tragically as a toddler. Ferdinand Herff and his wife would eventually rest there too. Their gravestones can be found in San Antonio City Cemetery No. 1.

How exactly Herff family members first came into possession of the three drawings is not recorded. It is easy to imagine that Friedrich made gifts of them to Ferdinand Herff over the years, or perhaps Herff acquired them from his deceased friend's estate. It is also reasonable to think that for Ferdinand Herff, the images were poignant reminders of his frontier days and his longtime friend, especially resonant since he lost his friend, as he had his little son, under heartbreaking circumstances. In any case, we are fortunate that he and his descendants preserved these drawings, for they are heirlooms in the rich legacy of German Texas and the Herff family, and testimonials to "loyalty and brotherly love."

Along with his many other pursuits, Friedrich cultivated his skills as an artist. A person with Friedrich's class position and level of education at the time could well be expected to have developed some talent with pencil or brush and to be familiar with fine art conventions. Moreover, his curriculum at the Darmstadt vocational school had a heavy emphasis on drawing. He was not alone among the Forty in possessing such aptitudes, as Charles Backofen, principally a builder of musical instruments, was also an able artist and, later, photographer (Hertzberg and Schenck 1988, 144; Reichstein 2001, 54). And among the German settlers were other accomplished and well-known artists whose works contribute to historical knowledge, and who are the usual suspects when new works from the Fredericksburg area are found. Friedrich Richard Petri (1824–1857) excelled in sketches and watercolors of human figures and domestic scenes (Newcomb and Carnahan 1978; Wickham 1997). Petri's brother-in-law and fellow student at the Royal Academy of Fine Arts in Dresden, Karl Friedrich Hermann Lungkwitz (1813–1891) also resided near Fredericksburg; he is celebrated for romantic landscapes in oil which evoke the Hudson River School, though he had no exposure to it (McGuire 1983). Carl G. von Iwonski (1830–1912) in New Braunfels and San Antonio was competent in many media, including painting, sculpture, and cartooning (McGuire 1976). Iwonski taught drawing at the San Antonio German-English School where Friedrich was a trustee. The French artist and surveyor Jean Louis Theodore Gentilz (1819–1906) produced several excellent paintings of Indians and other frontier subjects (Kendall and Perry 1974). Gentilz, first associated with the Castro colony south of Fredericksburg, befriended the Herffs in San Antonio—they were neighbors—and Friedrich probably knew him. Also in the area for a time was career U.S. Army officer Seth Eastman, a prolific sketch artist and painter (Burkhalter 1961; McDermott 1961; Lorbiecki 2000). All of these artists had formal training (except Iwonski, who may have had lessons from Petri and Lungkwitz) and commanded techniques of composition, figuration, and coloration not found in the drawings under consideration.[10]

Friedrich's hand is more that of a draftsman. He favors economy of line, and understands perspective but represents depth of field in a simple, mechanical manner. His human and animal figures are angular in shape and modular in execution; he is filling the blank paper to record his story, not displaying his grasp of technique for aesthetic purposes. Friedrich's style is matter-of-fact and exactly what we would expect from someone of his background and experience. Without subscribing to rigid classifications, it may be said that though they contain elements of elite art, Friedrich's sketches have qualities of both technical drawing and folk art. More will be said of Friedrich's artistic knowledge and technique as the drawings are interpreted.

CHAPTER THREE

MATERIALS, TECHNIQUES, AND COMPOSITION

Drawing 1 is densely illustrated on plain paper with graphite pencil. Brisk outlines and details of figures are done with pencil point strokes; lighter vertical lines in the foreground indicate grass, and faint shading is added throughout with the side of the pencil lead to suggest contours as well as a light source from back left. Overall, the pencil strokes are fairly light. Drawing 2 exhibits some different technique and some darker and heavier lines owing to the use of pen and ink. There is much more energy devoted to grass and ground texture, much of the foreground having a stippled appearance. Concurrently, there is an absence of shading that would indicate either texture or lighting. Also, the trees and clouds in the background of D2 are drawn less delicately than those in D1. In D1, patience is evident as the artist experiments with more refined ways of representing slopes and banks in the landscape; his effort is noticeable upon comparing the spectator's dangling legs and the line of riders descending from the upper right that appear in both drawings. Drawing 2 is done like D1 on plain paper, but with creases showing that it had once been folded three times, into one eighth of its full size. Drawing 3 is done on blue-lined paper resembling the ledger book paper used later by Plains Indian artists.

Its composition is much more open than that of D1, but otherwise the array of techniques appears the same, noticeable in the rendering of such details as the Indians' lances and the distant trees and clouds.

Even though D1 and D2 present essentially the same scene, there are some notable differences in how the scene is constructed. In D1 the main action with its befeathered Indian presenting a girl captive is placed near the center of the picture, while in D2 this activity is on the far left. Drawing 1 contains contrasting motion, with the slow patient progress of the travois, the milling of the horse herd, and stationary mounted warrior figures, but it still appears oddly placid or static compared to D2, where more vigorous motion is rendered at the focal point of the captive exchange. Neither D1 or D2 is quite as dependent as D3 on the landscape for telling its story. The far and near "mountains" (as karstic plateaus are called in the Hill Country) framing the wagon trail in D3, and the altitude of the Indians' lookout, are more fundamental to the story than the landscapes in D1 and D2. And there is motion to a far horizon, by the wagon train, but also echoed by some of the Indian riders, and thus suggestions of progress and destination not found in the other drawings.

Each of the three drawings is composed in three horizontal panels: foreground, middle ground, and background. This organization is common in European academic art and also found in its manifestations in Texas. It was employed, for example, by Lungkwitz (McGuire 1983, 58–59). Indeed, the earliest easel painting of an historical event in Texas, *The Destruction of the Mission San Sabá* completed in Mexico in the 1760s, which coincidentally involves Comanches at a location within the Fisher-Miller Grant, uses this same basic configuration, though with several important differences (Ratcliffe 1991). Tripartite composition aids the intent of narration by sorting the visual information into a main or focal area plus adjacent areas of contextualization, one immediate and the other distant from the viewer. As employed in the Romantic tradition, this manner of composition draws the eye from an arresting natural feature, human or animal figure, or scene of activity, deeper into the visual context, and thus supposedly further into contemplation about the place or event that has been illustrated. Tripartite organization is most perfectly realized in D3, with its pioneer wagon train in the middle, surveilling Indians in the foreground, and wilderness in the background. Furthermore, D3 resembles the images of "devout, happy figures along a road leading to distant mountains" that were standard fare in the late-romantic Dresden school that lurks as an influence on Friedrich (McGuire 1983, 59). In D1 and D2, however, there is some compositional ambiguity. In these drawings it is possible to discern closer and farther zones within the middle ground. And it is uncertain whether the most intense action, the exchange of the captive, really lies in the middle ground at all, or instead in the foreground; viewers can reasonably interpret the organization either way, and well might favor the "foregrounding" of the captive story. Whether this play was intentional on Friedrich's part is not known. Ultimately, these sketches still function to guide the eye and prioritize between subject and context much as they would if organized in the simpler three-part fashion.

CHAPTER FOUR
The Germans

The non-Indian men are readily identifiable as German settlers because of their uniform depiction with long beards. In this period, as a rule, beards distinguished the Germans from Anglos (e.g., Jordan 1976–77, 56, 61-62). The Penatekas seized upon Meusebach's long red beard as his defining feature (Tiling 1913, 84–85). The Forty settler Louis Reinhardt recalled that when he met the Penateka headman Santa Anna, the chief "was very much puzzled, too, because I had no beard; for all our party wore them. I told him with my fingers that I was only seventeen. Doubtless he had at first taken me for an American, as none of them wore beards at this time" (Reinhardt 1899, 38). Reinhardt's companion at Bettina Friedrich Schenck wrote to his mother in Germany in November 1847 that the "brown sons of the wilderness" referred to the Germans as "beardmen" (Hertzberg and Schenck 1988, 161). This term is probably a gloss of the Comanche word motsotaibo, "bearded white man"; this is an old theme in tribal culture, with a song and various stories about the wonder experienced when the Comanches, who typically plucked what little facial hair they had, saw men with beards for the first time.[1]

Along with beards, brimmed hats serve as unfailing metonyms for the Germans. Their uniform presence is remarkable if unlikely, and lends once again a stamp-like character to the imagery. This convention mirrors Indian practice, though not knowingly, for among the Comanches and other Southern Plains Indians, the brimmed hat was the symbol for a white man, whether in pictography or sign language; this seems to have been an extension of the Indian practice of symbolizing tribal affiliation by hairstyle (Clark 1982, 402-403; Gelo 1995, xxiii). And along with hats, the men all wear standardized pocketed coats, and trousers extending down to their shoes, except for a few whose pants are tucked into their boots—a detail repeated in both D1 and D2.

One more indication that the white men might be Germans appears in D3, for their wagons are drawn by oxen. With some exceptions, the Hill Country Germans preferred oxen as draft animals, while Anglo settlers more frequently used horses or mules (Reinhardt 1899, 35-36; Jordan 1966, 142, 194; cf. Roemer 1849, 274, 1983, 227; Reichstein 2001, 47). Oxen were cheaper and more reliable than equines and not significantly slower. Also, Indians were much less tempted to steal oxen than horses. Ernst Kapp told his relatives in Germany that "[t]he most aristocratic gentlemen drive ox-wagons here" (Spiess Papers, 112).

The Germans are engaged in several activities. Several of the men carry rifles, mostly leaning on them in a relaxed way. Many form a line as if waiting to greet the Indian chief. One man in line holds a dog by a long leash as some other dogs run about freely—this element is found in both D1 and D2. One or more Germans at the head of the line interact with the chief directly, and one in D2 only faces away with his arms raised, rifle in one hand, and seems to be making an announcement or hailing others who approach. A couple of Germans carry in a slain deer. In the lower left of D1, four men stand, squat, or lie as spectators. One gestures with his arm toward the central action while speaking to a woman, whose style of dress indicates that she is the only white woman in any of the three pictures, as if he is explaining what is going on. The woman wears a long dress with bell-shaped sleeves that became fashionable in the late 1840s; instead of a bonnet, a hat with round crown not unlike those of some of the men but decorated with a flowing scarf; long braids tied with ribbons; and she holds a rifle. The hat crowns of three of the men in lower left D1 are rounded rather than square, and there is a vague chance that this detail is intended to indicate a sombrero and hence a Mexican person. In D2 the hat crowns are not so distinctly shaped.

CHAPTER FIVE

COMANCHES AND THEIR HORSES

It is a foregone conclusion that the Indians in the drawings are Comanches, from their dominant position among area tribes, their known interactions with the Germans, and from details of dress and behavior, even though these include some imprecisions. It can be further stipulated that they are members of the Penateka division endemic to the area. Their attire and horsemanship cast them as a high plains tribe, distinct from the transplanted, acculturated eastern Delawares and Shawnees who guided the German pioneers. Lipan Apaches, Tonkawas, and Wichitans also frequented the area and would have resembled the Comanches in dress, but they were practically client populations of the Penatekas at this time, and were unlikely to have been a majority of the Indian participants in events of the scale depicted.

The Indians are drawn in the same way for the most part. The men are bare-legged, not wearing leggings, just breechclouts. Their breechclouts, and their upright head feathers which seem sometimes to be held in headbands in D1, are not particularly realistic, and often look more like the detailing seen on map cartouche Indians. No shirts, leather armor, or hair pipe breastplates are shown, and only one man wears leggings. Almost all the men hold lances; the long lance with wooden shaft and metal point, often fashioned from a sword blade, was a prominent Comanche weapon during the period (e.g., Dodge 1882, 421; Wallace and Hoebel 1952, 110–111). In both D1 and D2 one Indian man stands with his lance, his back turned to the viewer. In D1, left near middle ground, one of the Indians near the end of the mounted ranks is waving ribbons or streamers above his head with his right hand while holding up a lance with a skin or flag affixed to its end with his left hand. He appears to be signaling the other mounted Indians to ride in or assume a formation. Similar signaling with ribbons is performed by three men in D3, while three others make signals by holding their lances aloft. Such communications were part of a large repertoire of long-distance signaling methods that also included fire, smoke, blankets, skins, bird bone whistles, gestures with the shield or hand, and tight horse maneuvers. All these kinds of signals were typically sent from high ground as in D3 (e.g., Parker 1856, 142; Marcy 1866, 132; Hunter 1924, 13–14; Wilbarger 1985, 668). It is also possible that the skin or flag on the lance in D1 is a white one, as the Comanches were familiar with this conventional European peace signal and displayed it when greeting the Germans and other parties of white men (e.g., Catlin, 1973, plate 157 ff. p. 52; Penniger 1896, 90; 1971, 39; 2020, 123–24; Roemer 1848, 321; 1983, 266; Wilbarger 1985, 256; DeShields 1993, 155).

Seven Indian riders in D3 can be seen wearing quivers on their backs, and quivers are also discernable on at least four of the men in D1 and one man in D2. The quivers are rendered in a repeated fashion, and in their simplicity and positioning these are another cartouche-like detail. They look like relatively short, simple cylinders that do not project below the waist, worn on a slight slant, and often but not always with the top opening behind the wearer's right shoulder, in stereotypic Robin Hood style. Short Comanche quivers are not unknown, but they typically wore longer combination cases holding both the bow and arrows in adjoining sleeves (e.g., Berlandier 1969, 169, 173, 174). These were carried, at least when on horseback, more or less across the small of the back, with the arrow opening to the left (unless the warrior was left-handed), so they could be swung under the left arm or completely in front to draw arrows quickly while riding. "This is a little detail that few artists have observed correctly. Knowing only the English style, the majority of artists picture the Indian quiver backwards—or else they always draw left-handed Indians!" (Laubin and Laubin 1980, 128; see also Newcomb and Carnahan 1978, 132, plates 32–34 ff. p. 159).

One or more of the human figures at the extreme right near middle of D1 appear from their shape and status as casual spectators to be females. By extension one or two of the figures in a similar position in D2 could also be women. There is nothing, however, about the clothing of these figures that distinguishes them as female; Comanche women of the period wore dresses. In addition, close examination of D1 shows that these people wear feathers like men, and some hold lances and wear quivers. The most prominent of these is the figure lounging odalisque-like in D1, whose pose appears feminine if only because of western artistic convention. We are reminded of other examples of this colonialist trope, such as Louis Choris's circa 1826 lithograph of European explorers meeting King Tamméaméa (Kamehameha I) in 1816, with its demure (though not quite reclining) women perched on rocks and watching the proceedings (Chamisso 2012, 206; Figure 6). Friedrich's and Choris's figures in turn resemble the young women on the island of death in English artist William Etty's 1837 controversial oil *The Sirens and Ulysses* (Farr 1958, 67-68, 78-79, plates 62a, 63; Figure 7). The three situations represented in these works—the Forty's journey to the Texas wilderness, the voyage of the *Rurik* through the Pacific, and the Odyssey—are ripe for comparison. But it is impossible to say if Friedrich intended to provoke such comparisons or if he was merely caught up in a subliminal way in the artistic zeitgeist; or if, perhaps, the resemblances are nothing more than interesting coincidences.

Whether female or not, the reclining figure in D1 and its companions face the main activity in the center and direct attention to it. In this function they are balanced on the other side of the drawing by the man holding his horse and leaning nonchalantly against the tree. He also has an oddly affected posture and serves as a kind of framing figure

Figure 6. Lithograph of European explorers from the Russian ship *Rurik* meeting King Tamméaméa in 1816 by Louis Choris (circa 1826).

Figure 7. *The Sirens and Ulysses* by William Etty (1837).

customary in the European art tradition. The white men and woman looking on in D1's lower left also contribute to this function. The one unequivocally female figure appearing in both D1 and D2 is that of the captive, discussed below.

The Indians' various activities in D1 and D2 together represent an inventory of all those typical of a large, bustling gathering. While some talk with the Germans or relax and look on, others (in D2) carry in game. More tend a herd of livestock (frisky, unsaddled paint horses in D2, docile horses or mules in D1); several form a perimeter of mounted men as if to assert control over the proceedings, and still others travel in the background. The numerous Indian men on horseback lined up and equally spaced, either at rest or marching in, impress with their discipline and refinement, appearing no less civilized than the

Germans in their orderly queue. Something like this comportment is described in historical accounts: "All the young warriors of the tribe, several hundred of them, dressed ready for a foray into Mexico, lined up on one side of their camping ground near the San Saba River, the squaws and children on the other" (King 1967, 115); ". . . on the right wing were the warriors divided in sections and each section had a chief; the left wing was formed by the women and children, also mounted" (Penniger 1896, 91; 1971, 39; 2020, 124).

The detailing of Comanche horsemanship, including the form of the animals, riding postures, and tack, is praiseworthy. The Indian horses are small relative to their riders, though sturdy, and care was taken to show spots on several of them, all characteristic of the paint horses preferred by the Comanches. White settlers and soldiers thought them inferior to their own breeds, "unsightly and small" in the words of Roemer (1849, 324; 1983, 268; see also Roe 1955, 170–171). The horses are quick and graceful, their riders alternately stately or athletic. Drawing 3 is most notable in recording one of the riding stunts for which the Comanches were renowned, as two riders stand balanced on their horse's backs. Some of the horses have saddles or saddle pads. The horse with splayed legs in D1 has the most detailed saddle. Adept penciling shows girths in both front and rear positions (but no fenders or stirrups) and a small simple seat with high cantle and pommel, indicating a saddle of Spanish-Mexican design, or Indian-made on the Mexican model. The other Indian saddles match this style.

On many of the horses, Friedrich took special care to draw a long rope trailing from the jaw; this was obviously an important detail for him. This is a characteristic piece of Plains Indian tack known as a war rein or war bridle, and Friedrich was astute in including it. The war rein was a single buffalo hair or rawhide rope tied around the bars in the horse's lower jaw, forming what is known as a jaw-loop bridle (Mails 1995, 223-26; Martin, Martin, and Bauver 2010, 30–31; Cowdrey, Martina, and Martin 2012, 11, 28, 32, 109). Held by the rider alongside the horse's neck, the rope was used as a rein to control the animal's movements, but while galloping it could be dropped and allowed to drag so that the rider would have something to grab if he became dismounted. Comanches trained their horses with the war rein dangling so they would learn to avoid stepping on it. The knowledgeable frontier artist George Catlin (1796–1872) drew a somewhat similar Comanche system in *Comanche Meeting the Dragoons* (Figure 8), where the rider holds a single rein that looks like it is tied on the horse's lower jaw

Figure 8. *Comanche Meeting the Dragoons* by George Catlin (circa 1834).

Figure 9. Horse with Comanche-style jaw loop and saddle. Courtesy C. B. "Hoppy" Hopkins.

(though Catlin's prose description says it was tied to a heavy Spanish bit), with a separate long rescue rope tied to the horse's neck loop and trailing far behind. The neck loop was woven into the mane at either end and allowed the rider to suspend himself behind or under the neck while fighting (Catlin 1973, opp. 53, 56; Cowdrey, Martin, and Martin 2012, 54). Frederic Remington was another well-informed painter who illustrated the single war rein (Shapiro and Hassrick 1991, 124). Elsewhere, as in his 1834–35 oil *Comanche Feats of Horsemanship*, Catlin shows loop or tied split reins in use, though still just tied on the horse's lower jaw (Catlin 1973, opp. 65). This variation, but with the reins untied, as illustrated in Figure 9, is possibly shown by Friedrich in D1 on the riderless horse with splayed legs; the Indian behind this horse, with his back to viewers, holds the horse to his left with dual reins also. Friedrich shows another Comanche tack variation in D3, where the man wearing a warbonnet and his companion peering over the ridge appear to handle split reins attached to hackamores or bosals (nosebands).

Except for Catlin, Friedrich is alone among artists of the antebellum period in devoting so much attention to Comanche horses. Beyond the technical detail, he captures Comanche symbiosis with the animal and hints at the affection that individuals felt for their horses. As frontier chronicler Josiah Gregg observed, "Like [the Arabs], they dote upon their steeds; one had as well undertake to purchase a Comanche's child as his favorite riding-horse" (quoted in Roe 1955, 264). Gregg's comparison is suggestive given that Friedrich's main subject in D1 and D2 is the exchange of a young captive.

None of the livestock appears to belong to the Germans, with the important exception of the wagon train animals in D3. Here is fine detail of a driver with his whip resembling a modern longe whip, with equal-length shaft and lash, held high as he walks along with the oxen while his horse is led by another rider. One can see his empty saddle with its low broad horn and sloping cantle that suggest, whether intentionally or not, a Hope saddle, a forerunner of the western-style saddle developed in Texas in the 1830s and commonly used there afterwards.

CHAPTER SIX

ℱOREGROUND AND ℬACKGROUND

Both the lowest and highest thirds of Friedrich's three drawings are full of useful information. Along the bottom of D1 are several names and initials printed in capital Latin letters in pencil, some vertically and some horizontally, that appear to refer to the figures immediately above, and which we examine from left to right. All the printing looks to be in the same hand, and since the first two names are integral to human figures, all appears to have been inserted by the artist as he drew, not by him or someone else later. Almost imperceptible along the bottom of the woman's skirt are some indistinguishable letters,

perhaps four, followed by "HERF." No doubt this indicates that the woman depicted is Julie Herf, the lone adult female among the Bettina settlers. Herf (no relation to Ferdinand Herff) was a German woman from Baden who had previously traveled in America and become fluent in English; she signed on with the Forty as cook, housekeeper, and translator in Hamburg, and went to live with them at the commune (Reichstein 2001, 43).[1] A name of six letters next appears under the man to her right, across the end of his rifle stock, but it is so obscure as to discourage even an educated guess.

Under one of the large dead birds and below the German man standing just left of the Indian chief is the clear word "PICKER." Toward the right corner of the drawing are found horizontal letters "UBR" and the vertical "SCHWARTZE" (*sic*) and "MOPS." The first three remain mysterious, with no cognate initials or names in the written records. Interpreting "picker" as a noun and consulting German terms referring to blackness also proved fruitless. Nor is it possible to say which figures above these words correspond to them. It is tempting to propose that "MOPS" is the senior German settler in Sisterdale, Texas in 1853, whom Friedrich Kapp mentions by this name in his 1855 essay evaluating the Adelsverein and Texas settlements (Kapp 1876, 287; cf.

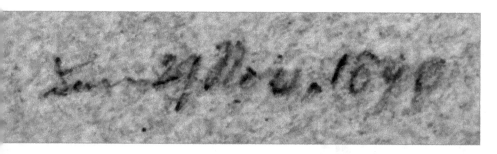

Figure 10. Close-up of Drawing 1 lower right corner showing vertical date.

Biesele 1930, 196). In German, however, the word "Mops" indicates a pug dog or a dog nickname akin to "Fido" among English speakers, and so the lettering probably just corresponds to the dog depicted above it. Fortier Louis Reinhardt remembered: "We had...a great many dogs of whom Morro was the largest, being three feet high" (Reinhardt 1899, 36). Ferdinand Herff wrote that they had 10 dogs, which lived well because wild meat was plentiful (Herff 1848:40, column 629). Another source maintains that the foresters brought fifteen hunting dogs and were upset when they had to pay extra for their passage (Heinemann 1994, 309).

In the lower right corner of D1, distinct from the block capital names and initials, is a vertical script date (Figure 10). Lax penmanship and foxing make some of this writing difficult to read; there is the German article *den* ("the"), as often precedes a date, followed by a two-digit date starting with "2" and second digit uncertain, though probably a 7, followed by "Nov. 184_." The last digit of the year is obscure, most likely a 7 or 9, perhaps an 8. This inscription appears to be the source of the date 1849 noted on the back of the drawing, but it is not immediately clear whether the date is meant to denote the day of the event portrayed, or when it was drawn, or when it was presented to someone.

Figure 11. Close-up of Drawing 3 bottom right corner showing legend.

No comparable "legend" writing appears in D2 apart from the artist's name and date in the lower right corner. Drawing 3 has a legend in its bottom right corner that is much worn, possibly partly rewritten, but still refreshingly understandable (Figure 11). In all probability it reads: "Auf dem Wege zum Rio Llano, den 25ten Sept. 1848. Friedrich" ("On the way to the Rio Llano, Sept. 25, 1848. Friedrich"). Otherwise, the foreground of D3 is special in offering a scene of action that parallels the one in its central section, and this feature is best discussed along with the middle section, below.

The other noteworthy aspect of the foregrounding is the depiction of slain animals in D1 and D2, developed a bit differently in each. In D1, the animals in the middle of the array are out of proportion, overly large in comparison to the humans near them, as if to emphasize them. Several of the animals have their bellies slit open—they have been field dressed, provided for the occasion as food or peltry. Among them are turkeys, deer, rabbits or hares, and large and small javelinas. This catalog of native species continues in the background of D3, which is decorated with living animals, including bison (two of them butting heads), mustangs, deer, and a pack of ten loping wolves or coyotes perfectly if minutely rendered with the fewest pencil strokes necessary. Drawing 3 also populates the sky with three clusters of V-shaped soaring birds, an obligatory element which anyone in the Hill Country would interpret as ubiquitous turkey vultures. Friedrich's animal drawings are a complement to the lengthy descriptions of animal life that settlers frequently sent home in letters and notes, marveling at the plenitude, appearance, and behaviors of the different creatures; the Fortier Friedrich Schenck, for instance, told his mother "[t]he wealth of wildlife is indescribable," and Ferdinand Herff wrote "[t]here is no Bohemian wild-life preserve where you can see more deer than in some areas of the Texas prairie" (Hertzberg and Schenck 1988, 153–56; Herff 1848:40, column 629, translated by Wickham).

Of special interest to naturalists is the depiction of two slain large spotted cats in Drawings 1 and 2 which can only be jaguars. It is not commonly known that this species ranged so far northward in times past, but there are several written accounts of jaguars in Texas from the mid-nineteenth century (Weniger 1997, 79–84; Robinson 2006, 3–4). Anglo Texans at the time usually referred to these big cats as "tigers," consistent with the American Spanish "tigre," or sometimes as "leopards," a term more often used for ocelots, and they were clearly distinguished from "panthers" or mountain lions. Among those recording the presence of jaguars in Texas during the 1840s and 1850s were the naturalist John James Audubon, Smithsonian scientist Spencer F. Baird, and U.S. Army explorer A. W. Whipple. Audubon interviewed Texas Ranger captain and surveyor Jack Hays in San Antonio in 1845 about his many encounters with jaguars, and Sam Houston told Audubon that the big cats had been found on the upper Guadalupe and San Marcos Rivers (Audubon and Bachman 1854, 4–6).

Some of the best jaguar information comes from men associated with the German and Alsatian settlements. Viktor Bracht, extolling the wonders of Texas in 1848, mentions "the beautifully spotted American tiger, or jaguar," "the handsomest native animal," rare, but most common between the Medina and the Rio Grande (Bracht 1931, 43, 183). That same year the Abbé Domenech heard "the caterwaulings of panthers and tiger-cats" while camped west of San Antonio (Domenech 1858, 143). Ferdinand Roemer's observations, buried in an appendix never published in English translation, are especially pertinent because he was a member of the Meusebach Treaty party, a trained geologist serving as naturalist for the expedition (Roemer 1849, 462–64). Roemer wrote that in the 1840s several jaguars were shot around San Antonio, their pelts fetching $18 apiece. He saw Comanche men wearing jaguar skin bowcase/quivers, which would have been an upgrade from the usual deer hide or mountain lion skin. Observing in 1849, Wilhelm Steinert seconded Roemer's report: "We saw jaguar skins with the Indians. Panthers occurred likewise" (Steinert 1850, 182). Describing the headman of a troop of Comanches visiting Fort Martin Scott, Steinert wrote, "His arrows were stuck in a beautiful quiver made of tiger skin which he wore on his back" (Jordan 1976–77, 118). But for Roemer and Steinert, Comanche jaguar skin quivers would be unknown to the ethnographic record. In a December 25, 1851, letter to family in Germany, settler Franz Kettner mentions the hunting adventures of his business partner Emil Kriewitz: "What is quite rare is that a short time ago Kriewitz shot a magnificent spotted tiger cat" ("eine prachtvoll gefleckte Tigerkatze") (Wurster 2008, 34, 40). A jaguar was shot near London, Kimble County, formerly in the Fisher-Miller Grant, in 1909. Photos exist of this animal and three others of the five known jaguars slain in Texas between 1903 and 1948 (see DuBois 2020). But unless Audubon collected a specimen for painting in Texas, and it appears rather his models were two zoo animals in Charleston, South Carolina (see Audubon and Bachman 1854, 3, 7), Friedrich's drawings remain the only known pictorial evidence for jaguars in Texas prior to the twentieth century.

Another species that is probably represented is the wapiti or elk (*Cervus canadensis*), which might be distinguished from deer in the pictures by their larger antlers. There has been some disagreement about whether elk were native to Texas, but again we have confirmation in nineteenth-century writings, and there is also evidence in archaeological remains and Indian pictography (Weniger 1997, 46–51; Gill et al. 2016). Bracht, Roemer, and George Wilkins Kendall, among others, offered contemporary observations. Bracht commented, "It is said that there are elk and mountain sheep in the northern part of Texas. I have never seen any" (Bracht 1931, 42); Kendall wrote that in 1841 the Brazos valley "teemed with every species of game," including elk (Kendall 2004, 51). There are also the two 1846–1848 oils by Catlin entitled *Elk and Buffalo Grazing among Prairie Flowers, Texas* and *Buffalo and Elk Making Acquaintance in Texas* (Smithsonian America Art Museum acc. no. 1985.66.580, 1985.66.581). Judging from the reports, elk were not abundant in the historic period, and more likely to be found in the extreme northern or southern parts of the state rather than in the central area where the Germans settled.

These animals—deer, hares (jackrabbits), wild turkeys, javelinas, wolves, jaguars, elk—have interesting symbolic value, because they are all, to the Germans, new species or subspecies that are members of genera known in the Old World. They are thus both familiar and exotic. Schenck wrote at length comparing the Texas animals with those he knew from home (Hertzberg and Schenck 1988, 153-56). The animals were also a potent representation of the natural world that the Germans would need to conquer. As Schenck told his mother, "This land, upon which a few weeks ago, only buffalo, lions, wolves, and panthers confronted each other, is becoming transformed into a harmonious

countryside" (Hertzberg and Schenck 1988, 149-150). That operation
is underway in D2, which shows slain deer being brought in by both
Indians and Germans. The immediate intention here, though, is not to
tame the wilderness, but to mount a feast of goodwill.[2]

The great variety of wildlife lends a feel not unlike that of the
Peaceable Kingdom paintings by contemporary American folk artist
Edward Hicks (1780–1849), even if some of Friedrich's animals
are fighting and others dead. Hick's Quaker pacifist ideology was
expressed not only in biblical imagery of lions lying with lambs (and
oxen and children), but with depictions of Native Americans meeting
William Penn, inspired by Benjamin West's 1771-72 oil painting *The
Treaty of Penn with the Indians* (Ford 1998). Friedrich even added a
large serpent in the lower right corner of D2. Like the other figures that
dutifully face the main action, the snake slithers left and upwards. It is
tempting to suppose that this is a rattlesnake, as they are the common
scourge of the country, but it lacks any of the necessary detail. Its
dark, even coloration suggests another pervasive large serpent, one
with a cultural connection: the rat snake (*Elaphe obsoleta*; Roemer's
"chicken snake" [1849, 173; 1983, 140]). The Texas subspecies (*E. o.
lindheimeri*) is named for Ferdinand Jacob Lindheimer, a celebrated
German immigrant naturalist and associate of Herff and others in
the colonist community, who along with Emil Kriewitz guided the
Bettina settlers to their land. The Fortiers welcomed Lindheimer at
Bettina because of his experience in Texas and with Indians, and he
stayed with them for the first month (Lindheimer 1848, column 778;
Heinemann 1994, 319).

Though richly symbolic, the hunted animals present an anomaly, for
some of them are provided by the Germans, and there is mixed evidence

on the inclination and competence of the Germans settlers as hunters (e.g., Roemer 1849, 175–76; 1983, 141–42; Smithwick 1983, 227; Wurster 2008, 34, 40; Lindheimer 1879, 10–12; Williams 2020, 19–21). The Forty were expected to keep themselves well-armed and to be proficient with firearms, to attack or defend against Indians (Heinemann 1994, 290–91, 309, 324). But it is fair to say that with more than a few exceptions (like the foresters with their hunting dogs, or Kriewitz and his jaguar), compared to the "Americans" the early German colonists were not strongly disposed to hunting, in part because in Germany it had become an activity reserved for the privileged classes. Roemer shot some game on the Meusebach expedition, but the leader had contracted with Shawnee hunters to feed the party, and Delaware guide Jim Shaw supplied some meat as well. Adding to this quandary, the Comanches visiting the Germans were frequently ravenous and dependent on the food stores of their hosts. Their condition reflects multiple factors, including the reduction of the buffalo, the scarcity of game in winter, and Indian expectations of hospitality. Thus, both Germans and Comanches depended on the hunting of the Indian guides during their earliest meetings; perhaps later, at Bettina, either or both brought more to the table or to trade. Friedrich's pictures suggest that both principal groups are staging a collective feast, with their contributions laid out on display. This representation is probably idealized, corresponding to the Peaceable Kingdom motif and other idyllic aspects of the drawings.

Along with the animals in the background in D1 and D2 are human figures, rendered exquisitely in miniature with single strokes and dots to show critical detail. We see lines of travois (more carefully drawn in D1), mule-drawn A-frame drags that the Comanches used to transport their tipi poles, folded tipi covers, and sundry worldly possessions packed in rawhide suitcases called parfleches. The travois are proceeding in single file, and their gentle pace contrasts with both the frenetic riding and stationary mounts shown elsewhere in the pictures. Each travois mule in D1 has multiple children perched on its back and is led by a woman who is the caretaker of the children and owner of the household goods, exactly as Comanches would have traveled while moving camp. Other children travel alongside on foot, several with arms akimbo, in play. Immediately beyond the travois line and traveling in the same direction is a string of mules or horses led by a mounted man; then files of mounted warriors parading into the scene in the same direction. These details call to mind descriptions from the Meusebach expedition on February 7, 1847: "…a large number of Indians in their colorful array came down the hill in formation"; "On the evening of this day almost the entire [Comanche] village came storming over to our camp, creating a terrible noise, because everyone, including small children, rode horseback, three and four children on one horse" (Penniger 1896, 91, 93; 1971, 39, 40; 2020, 125, 127). Through their manner of execution and position in the picture these distant people are assimilated to nature—they are moving through the background or inward from it, part of the natural environment that the Germans were learning to deal with.

Friedrich's portrayal of the land and its vegetation is essential to the composition, yet largely devoid of symbolic, narrative, or historical information. Nothing like the rocks signifying faith, prevalent in the paintings Lungkwitz (McGuire 1983, 57), is seen in Friedrich's sketches. Notable area landmarks like Enchanted Rock and House Mountain are absent. There is a large leafy tree at left in D1 that corresponds to similar trees in the distance. Similar trees are only hinted at in D2, only in the background. Trees of this size and growth habit in the area are generally oaks or cedar elms, perhaps hackberries; but the rendering of the leaves appears perfunctory, and so Friedrich ignores an opportunity to impart some specific information, not only about the species but also the time of year, for Texas live oaks shed their leaves in spring. The most that might be said symbolically of the large tree in D1 is that it is a shade tree evoking the comforts of settlement. In this function it corresponds to the nearby stone wall, but the wall has other, historical implications that must be examined below. Some distinctive details in the background of D1 and D2 concerning the slope of the land do seem purposeful and must also be interpreted below against historical accounts.

CHAPTER SEVEN

MAIN ACTION

The main action in D1 and D2 involves an Indian man standing behind and holding a girl in Indian dress. The man is a chief (band headman), indicated by his full-feather warbonnet—he is the only person wearing one. The feathers, from the immature golden eagle, each stand for a brave deed, advertising the wearer's war record, in this case a highly distinguished one. This style of headdress, with one or two long trailers extending from the back of the crown, down the wearer's back to his heels, is historically significant. It is generally thought that Comanches rarely wore feather warbonnets of any kind before the reservation period of the late 1800s. It might be supposed that they acquired the warbonnet following from their alliance with the Cheyennes and Arapahos in winter 1839–1840, and that they adopted the elaborate trailer style from Cheyenne and Sioux practice only in the later nineteenth century (see Wallace and Hoebel 1952, 82–83). The tradition of wearing captured enemy regalia as battle trophy meant that the warbonnet could have diffused to the Comanches in this way also. Comanche oral history holds that the warrior Piatutakoniwap wore some kind of eagle-feather warbonnet during the September 1872 Battle of the North Fork of Red River (Attocknie 2016, 122). A long trailer bonnet purported to have been worn by Quanah Parker at the 1874 Adobe Walls battle is preserved in the Lowie Museum of Anthropology at the University of California, Berkeley (Baker and Harrison 1986, Figure 23 ff. p. 42). Tantalizing evidence of trailer bonnets for the same period or earlier is also found the El Caido site in northern Coahuila, where three images of a man with this style headgear are incised and overpainted in red pigment on a rock shelter wall; the images have been interpreted as a combat biography, possibly referring to a nearby skirmish between the U.S. Army and Comanche and Kiowa raiders circa 1873 (Labadie et al. 1997). Comanche trailer bonnets also appear in photos of dances and parades from the late 1800s and thereafter (e.g., Noyes 1999, 50–51).

If Penatekas wore any headgear at all during Friedrich's era, beyond one or a few decorative feathers, it was usually a cap of wooly buffalo hide with buffalo horns attached on either side, either the actual buffalo scalp or a facsimile (Burnet 1851, 234). Meusebach Treaty eyewitness Ferdinand Roemer observed "a peculiar headdress made of buffalo skin with the horns of the buffalo fastened to it" among the "war emblems" staged outside of the Comanche lodges (Roemer 1849, 322; 1983, 267). Two anonymous participants on the expedition went a step further, noting who was eligible to wear the bison scalp: "the chief's and the first warrior's headdress is the head hide of the buffalo with the horns of the animal attached" (Penniger 1896, 92; 1971, 39; 2020, 125).

Sometime between 1828 and 1851, however, the French-Mexican naturalist Jean Louis Berlandier collected a Comanche trailer war-bonnet in Texas that now resides in the Smithsonian. This item differs in some construction details from later parade bonnets, for example, lacking a pronounced visor-like brow band, but it clearly resembles the one that Friedrich drew. Smithsonian ethnologist John Ewers noted that Wyoming Shoshonis, from whom the Comanches were an offshoot, wore similar headdresses in the 1830s (Berlandier 1969, 177-80). Moreover, a watercolor by Lino Sánchez y Tapia painted prior to 1839 and based on a Berlandier field sketch from 1828 illustrates one Comanche man with a buffalo scalp headdress and a second with a trailer warbonnet (Berlandier 1969, 154, 157, 180; plate 3 ff. p. 164). To make matters more complicated, a feather bonnet with horns was collected after a Comanche raid on Corpus Christi in 1844 and drawn by William Bollaert, and two combination bonnets like this were painted at the El Caido rock shelter site (Berlandier 1969, 169; Labadie et al. 1997, 19, 20, 22). A splendid example of the feather and horn bonnet is worn by an unidentified Comanche warrior at Fort Sill, Indian Territory, in a photo portrait by William P. Bliss dated 1874 (Jones 2014, 105). Therefore, Comanches used a variety of headgear and knew some form of the trailer warbonnet during Friedrich's time, but it was uncommon, and not mentioned in the writings of the German chroniclers.

Corresponding to the warbonnet is a medallion hanging around the chief's neck, no doubt a peace medal of the kind presented to Indian leaders by various governments and companies, proudly worn as a status symbol. The chief also wears fringed leggings in both drawings, held by a belt in D1. It appears he is shirtless. The man's right braid is shown in D1.

The chief's identity is open to informed speculation. Roemer famously described the appearance of the Penateka headmen, saying that Old Owl was "undistinguished" in his dirty cotton jacket, while

Santa Anna and Buffalo Hump were different, the latter "genuine," scorning European clothing, and going naked above the waist with his long black hair hanging down (Roemer 1849, 324; 1983, 269). Unfortunately, he does not comment on their headgear. The chief's peace medal suggests he had been to visit Washington, D.C., and Roemer noted that Santa Anna had visited there just before his meetings with Meusebach (Roemer 1849, 321; 1983, 266). From among the twenty-four Comanches who signed the Butler and Lewis Treaty with the U.S. government on May 15, 1846, Old Owl, Buffalo Hump, and Santa Anna were selected to travel to Washington in July 1846 as part of a larger Indian delegation (Hughes 1846, 289, 352; Viola 1995, 20, 26, 55, 108, 123, 138; Kavanagh 1996, 296–301; Richardson 1996, 68–69). Of the Penatekas, only Santa Anna is known to have made the trip, during which he was received by President Polk and toured the Capitol Building (where he admired Catlin's Comanche paintings). Santa Anna referred to the visit in profound terms in his oration at the conclusion of the Meusebach Treaty Council (Penniger 1896, 106; 1971, 45; 2020, 141–42). It is likely, though not verified, that Santa Anna was given a presidential peace medal during this visit. He and the other Penateka leaders could have been given medals at the May treaty signing as well, or earlier, as medals, along with printed testimonials, canes, and flags, were common diplomatic gifts from all the colonial powers and private traders; so a medal in the drawing cannot prove the wearer's identity (see Roemer 1849, 294–95; 1983, 245; Penniger 1896, 100; 1971, 43; 2020, 135). Furthermore, Santa Anna was described as full-moon-faced and corpulent (Herff 1848:43, column 677; Heinemann 1994, 325), not at all like the trim chief in Friedrich's drawings. It is equally possible that Friedrich did not intend to draw a specific person but rather a conventionalized representation of Penateka leadership, in which case the warbonnet and peace medal are effective details. Both the bonnet and medal are icons that Friedrich could have seen first-hand or learned about from existing European and American artwork.

That the female is less than fully adult age is suggested by her height relative to the chief's: she rises about to his chest. She wears a dress with a full-length skirt, drawn with cross-hatching that seems to represent some decoration or texture. Her clothing differs from that of the one other woman, who is white, shown in D1 and appears to be an Indian dress.

The chief is in the posture of presenting the girl to the white men standing before them. In both drawings he holds her in a peculiar way, clutching her right wrist with his right hand and holding her arm up. Whereas in D1 he simply stands behind her as they both face the white men, in D2 some struggle is apparent. Here the girl is leaning backward with one foot off the ground, and her left arm is being held or pulled forward by another Indian. In both cases the nearest facing white man extends his arms toward the girl, but in D1 he stands or steps easily and appears to be examining her, while in D2 he strides and stretches forward as if to embrace or grab her, adding to the animation. It looks like the girl is being exchanged from the Indians to the whites, and therefore is either an Indian girl bestowed to the whites or an acculturated captive being turned over to them.

The first impression might be that the girl is Indian and is reluctant to become a present to the visitors. The corollary assumption might be that if she were a captive, she would be eager to escape from the Comanches and join the whites. The literature, however, contains many examples of captives who resisted rejoining white society once they had become assimilated as Indians (see Exley 2001, 135–138; Zesch 2004, 111–115; Rivaya-Martínez 2006, 291–94, 298). Those who were redeemed often drifted back to live with their former captors (Neighbours 1975, 186; Zesch 2004, 248-51), and when the Comanches were driven to reservations many captives chose to continue living among them (Rivaya-Martínez 2006, 298). It is likely that the girl in D2 is struggling to stay with the Indians, not leave them. Friedrich's drawing appears to show her rearing back from the white men, not straining towards them.

Less intense drama unfolds in D3, as a wagon train makes its way through a pass toward a hilly horizon at what appears to be a slow and steady pace. Six covered wagons are shown, each drawn by six spotted oxen. This placid, iconic image of western settlement is offset by the actions of the Indians in the foreground. Five Indian riders, including one wearing a trailer warbonnet, watch the train pass from higher ground. Another holds the reins of his horse as he approaches the brink of the elevation on foot, as if to peer over, though he appears to be signaling either his companions or the party below by waving his lance. Six more Indians ride along the high ground in the same direction as the wagon train and hail the Germans below. The positioning of the figures is an accurate depiction of Comanche reconnaissance and signaling methods. There is no indication that the Indians are attacking or preparing to attack, but rather offering a friendly greeting, of which the Germans are yet unaware.

CHAPTER 8

ᲤHE ᲛETTING

The date and location of the wagon train in D3 are posited with confidence if only because of the inscription bottom right explaining that the party shown is on its way to the Llano River in September 1848. This note is not automatically helpful, though, for in fact the Fortier migration to the Llano took place in September 1847. Given the tattered condition of this corner of the drawing, and what appears like fainter writing under the inscription now visible, it is probable that the inscription was written later in an attempt to repeat information that had become illegible or flaked away; at that point the mistaken date could have been introduced. Another possibility is that the piece was drawn by Friedrich in September 1848 and so signed with that date. This alternative is feasible because another date of 1848 can be seen remaining faintly near the torn paper edge, in what appears to be the same handwriting as the remedial inscription. It is not likely that the wagon train shown was one other than the migration train in question—one bringing supplies to the Llano colony a year later, say— because the settlement "went to pieces like a bubble," as Reinhardt put it, in less than a year (Reinhardt 1899, 39).

The landscape depicted fits well with historical accounts of the Fortiers' entrée (e.g., Heinemann 1994, 319–20). Kriewitz recollected that upon returning from his time among the Comanches, he was commissioned to "chart a road to the Llano and make it passable for wagons. After the road had been opened, the Darmstaedter colony arrived in Fredericksburg and I brought them to the place where Mr. A. Evers now lives and there they established their colony called Bettina" (Penniger 1896, 92; 1971, 49; 2020, 154). Kriewitz's commission came from Hermann Spiess, who later claimed, "I had a road laid out and kept in repair and prepared the river crossing—all for the expected Darmstadters—who also lent a hand with the road and the crossing" (Spiess Papers, 26). Kriewitz led his party across the river at Catfish Crossing near present Castell, Texas.[1] Castell lies twenty direct miles almost due north of Fredericksburg or thirty-nine miles on modern roads. It is hard to believe that Kriewitz cut a brand-new wagon road, even if he had the help of a large crew, in the supposed time frame. It is far more likely that he improved, where necessary, on an existing route. While still waiting to begin the trek in New Braunfels, Ferdinand Herff reported "the trail from Fredericksburg [to the Bettina site] is only 35 miles and is very good, communication with the rest of the world is not particularly difficult" (Herff 1848:45, column 705, translated by Wickham). Kriewitz would have led the settlers down the old Camino Real (King's Highway, Nacogdoches Road) segment southwest from New Braunfels to the outskirts of San Antonio, then headed northwest on the cut-off to the Pinta Trail running south of Comanche Springs, present Camp Bullis (see Reinhardt 1899, 37; Gelo and Wickham 2018, 76–77). With the Pinta Trail unsuitable for wagons, they would have jogged to the Camino San Saba running roughly parallel and about two miles to the west, including present Old Fredericksburg Road across the boundary of Bexar and Kendall Counties, and taking it north to reach Fredericksburg. From there, the path to the Llano crossing was some variation of the route presently covered by U.S. 87, and Keyserville Road, or FM 152. Catfish Crossing was a known Indian ford. In taking this route they repeated the southern segment of the path taken by Meusebach's treaty party (Sörgel 1992, 156–58, 338–340).[2] The trip from Fredericksburg to the commune site took fourteen hours according to one estimate (Reichstein 2001, 48–49). Mountain pass terrain resembling that shown in D3 is found along U.S. 87 between Hill Top and Cherry Spring.

The triumphant tone of the migration drawing echoes the feelings of the small group of young men upon completing their journey. "We came prepared to conquer the world," remembered Reinhardt (1899, 36). Though they suffered along the way, they felt they had beaten the odds. As Schenck boasted, "In Galveston, people prophesied to us the loss of half of our company! In Indian Point some went further and even wagered that not even half of the goals of our trip would be achieved, and that we could *not avoid our end!*" (Hertzberg and Schenck 1988, 149; emphasis in original). They even find that the looming Indians are not menacing but welcoming, once they become aware of them; in the drawing the Indians seem practically gleeful that the Germans are coming.

The Comanches' ability to secretly observe the Germans became evident from the first days of Meusebach's entrance into the trans-Llano country. "There was no doubt that we were being watched because the Shawnees assured us that we would be under continuous surveillance by the Comanches whose tracks they had observed" (Penniger 1896, 89; 1971, 38; 2020, 122). While the treaty party was still away from Fredericksburg, Old Owl and sixty warriors arrived in the town to inquire about the party's intentions, stating that he had followed the Germans, though unnoticed, ever since they crossed the Llano (Penniger 1896, 100; 1971, 43; 2020, 135).

Regardless of its historical basis, Friedrich's wagon train scene must be somewhat idealized. Though they pertain to the entire journey and not just the Fredericksburg-Bettina leg, the recollections of Fortiers Reinhardt and Schenck give a less tidy picture of the passage. Reinhardt, writing in old age, remembered at least twenty-four wagons, with mules as well as oxen for traction, needed for their "immense amount of baggage" (Reinhardt 1899, 35–36). Schenck wrote of ox-carts and pack trains as well as wagons, proceeding in divided small groups, and a slow-moving herd of cattle driven along (Hertzberg and Schenck 1988, 157–59).

Drawing 3 shares key motifs with another well-known work by a German-American artist. Emanuel Leutze's *Westward the Course of Empire Takes its Way* (1860) (Figure 12) also depicts a train of ox-drawn wagons negotiating mountainous country as they progress from right to left bringing settlers to new territories in the American west. And while in-depth comparison of Friedrich's pencil sketch with Leutze's operatic hymn to Manifest Destiny may be out of order, a brief look at Leutze's monumental mural, on display in the House wing of the Capitol in Washington, D.C., serves to direct our attention to some of the decisions (conscious or unconscious) that Friedrich faced as he composed his drawing.

Unlike Friedrich's, Leutze's travelers are depicted as individual men, women, children, and infants, grouped dramatically to show elements of their particular struggles and stories; the terrain in the mural depicts a wooded, rugged Rocky Mountain pass; while the emotional energy, lending an even more triumphant feel than is found in Friedrich's wagon train scene, is generated not least by enthusiastic gesticulation by the travelers' lookouts from their elevated perch as they catch sight of the promised land bathed in sunlight. The valley they have left is swathed in shadow and darkness. The allegorical intent is unambiguous, and the self-image of the Union at mid-century and its Eurocentric exceptionalism are on full display. Racial diversity is confined to one black youth leading a mule bearing a white woman and her baby. Indians are entirely absent, except that their smoke signals can be seen in the distance telegraphing news of the pioneers' approach.

By contrast, Friedrich's sketch demonstrates restraint. The terrain, though hilly, is not forbidding; the human figures with the wagons suggest token humanity and community, but we learn nothing about them as individuals; and the vegetation plays a role closer to that of benign observer than obstructive adversary. Most significantly, however, the point of view is that of the Natives in the foreground. The mounted Indians, the headman in his warbonnet, and the lookout on the rock join the viewer of the sketch in watching the slow progress of the train. Where Leutze's lookout belongs to the immigrants, stands on his rock, and is jubilant, Friedrich's is a Native who observes, cautiously, from behind a rock, signaling to his fellows or greeting the newcomers. In both cases, the job of the lookout might be interpreted as to see the future. The dynamism in Friedrich's sketch derives from the Comanche horsemen in the foreground, whose excitement might

Figure 12. *Westward the Course of Empire Takes Its Way* by Emanuel Leutze (1860).

arise from a welcoming impulse or from nervous apprehension at the strangers' arrival. In the background, on the far side of the trail, the wildlife provides a quiet pendant complementing the Indian energy and completing the context of already existing life the Germans are entering. Where Leutze seeks to draw the viewer into the drama to share the emotional experience of the immigrants, Friedrich offers a contemplative, distanced observer position mediated by the Indian surrogates, with whom the viewer is invited to identify.[3]

CHAPTER NINE

COMANCHE CAPTIVES

As in D3, the main action in D1 and D2 also corresponds to documented events, but the historical records provide at least two different captive exchange events as possible inspirations. The first of these to consider is an incident that took place during the Meusebach Treaty council. Roemer noted:

> We saw among the Comanches all kinds of moveable articles stolen in Mexico, such as costly blankets, mules, horses, harnesses, etc. We also saw captured Mexican men, women, and children. Several of these had lived for so long a time among the Indians that they had no desire to return to their native land; they were therefore not treated as prisoners. A young Mexican woman with whom her master was dissatisfied, was offered to us for the small sum of forty dollars. (Roemer 1849, 326; 1983, 271)

Roemer introduces this observation as an aside within his diary of the three-day treaty council, so the date is not clearly indicated. It most likely occurred on March 2, 1847, the full day of meeting, or perhaps on the morning of March 3, after the truce was set and the Germans were preparing to ride home.

The two anonymous participants who wrote about the treaty expedition lend credence to Roemer's observation. These "officers" later returned to Germany and published their recollections of the journey in a series for the *Magazin für die Literatur des Auslandes* beginning in August 1847, a mere five months after the adventure, reproduced in Penniger's 1896 Fredericksburg anniversary album and its later English editions (Anon. 1847; Penniger 1896, 86-107; 1971, 37-45; 2020, 119-142; 135). They stated that: "The cowardice of the Mexicans, to which the Comanches refer with great contempt, permits them to engage in the most daring exploits. Several of their children taken captive were offered us for very nominal ransom fees" (Penniger 1896, 98; 1971, 42; 2020, 133). This comment, like Roemer's, is offered retrospectively, so there is no further information about when the captives were proffered, or whether any of the offers were considered or accepted. The officers' commentary on the entire trip is both similar to and different from Roemer's, enough to engender confidence that theirs is a reliable, independent report.

Of the captive mentioned by Roemer, we do not know her name, or whether the Germans purchased her; there is no other mention of the young woman or the incident specifically in the annals of the Adelsverein.[1] Much of what was going on that day, however, can be deduced after considering Joaquín Rivaya-Martínez's outstanding study of Comanche captives (Rivaya-Martínez 2006, 278–298). In his sample of 773 documented captivities whose destiny is known, 40% of the captives were traded, ransomed, recovered, or escaped. Ten percent were ransomed, normally after arduous searches by their relatives or government authorities, and with the help of intermediaries. Less than 1% of those recovered were rescued against their will. Captives who resisted redemption were typically fearful of what their life would be like in white society, and some 15% were adopted into Comanche families, with marriage and property rights, and thus deeply assimilated. It was unusual for Comanches to give up a captive of their own initiative, and then almost always for a substantial ransom. They were only willing to surrender assimilated captives in rare circumstances, as when the captive's Comanche relatives all died, or there was a need to exchange for native-born Comanches held as prisoners by the Army. On a few occasions, Comanches offered captives as gifts of goodwill during treaty negotiations; two examples of this practice are recorded during their interactions with the Spanish (Rivaya-Martínez 2006, 295–96, 408). Such an offer was consistent with Indian principles of alliance, under which groups cemented a relationship by exchanging members.

None of these eventualities would have surprised the Germans, who were expecting to find captives during their Comanche encounters. Alwin Sörgel, in Fredericksburg during the Comanche visit there that occurred while Meusebach was heading north for his negotiations, wrote that the Indians were heading for Mexico and "ihre Beute an Kühen, Pferden, Weibern schon im Voraus feilbietend" ("offering in advance their booty of cattle, horses, and women"; Sörgel 1992, 159, 341). Meusebach's guide Lorenzo de la Rosa was a former captive; and the party met among the Indians eighteen-year-old blond Warren Lyons, taken captive in Austin ten years prior, who himself kept a little Mexican boy as his slave, and who refused the Germans' offer to take him back to the settlements. Another boy they met, a Comanche who spoke English, had been a prisoner of the whites in San Antonio after the Council House Fight (Roemer 1849, 292–93; 1983, 242–43; Zesch 2004, 28–29, 32). In February 1847, Emil Kriewitz told his mother half-jokingly that his only marriage prospect was to buy a captive Mexican woman from the Indians (Gelo and Wickham 2018, 114).

Since a treaty agreement, with its inherent need to establish lasting bonds, was the basis for the March convening, and since the ransom amount for the Mexican girl was only, in Roemer's words, a small sum, there is some reason to believe that the Germans redeemed the girl. On the other hand, a young Mexican woman may not have wanted to go with the German strangers. If they did acquire her, the Germans would have adopted her or attempted to reunite her with her Mexican family; a few years later some German traders tried unsuccessfully to ransom captive Juan Vela Benavides when he requested that they purchase him and send him home to Matamoros (Rivaya-Martínez 2006, 288, 515). But whether or not the transaction was completed, it should be understood as a counterpart to the arrangement by which German settler Emil Kriewitz would go to live with the Comanches (Gelo and Wickham 2018, 69–81). When and how exactly this pledge was made is not recorded, but it was clearly part of the Meusebach Treaty agreement. Soon after the council, Kriewitz began his stay of over three months among the Indians as an emissary, his presence securing the peace. He lived with Santa Anna, who regarded him as a potential son-in-law, and learned some of the Comanche language. In August 1847 Kriewitz slipped back to the settlements, afterwards serving as a guide and later as a merchant and postmaster. As noted earlier, it was Kriewitz who guided the Fortiers across the Llano to the site of their community.

But there were reportedly one or more other episodes involving the Germans and a Mexican Indian captive. These events are said to have taken place in Bettina or New Braunfels. The accounts vary and must be treated systematically to reconcile them.

CHAPTER TEN

THE GIRL

The most frequently repeated story has its origins in Herff family oral history; it has become a popular legend told to epitomize the friendly overtures made between the Bettina settlers and local Indians (Weber 1894, part 1, pages 30–31; Dielmann 1954, 274; Herff 1973, 12–15; King 1967, 122; Morgenthaler 2007, 80–81, 165). The story goes that within a few weeks after the colony was started, Ferdinand Herff had become known to the Comanches as a healer, and they brought him a man with advanced cataracts. Herff had the proper instruments to perform an extraction and took on the procedure with some ingenious measures to put the patient under and ensure the necessary lighting and cleanliness. The operation proved a complete success. As he was leaving, the overjoyed patient promised to bring Herff a wife. The Germans did not take his remark seriously, but about three months later the Comanche man reappeared and left a captive teen-aged Mexican girl. "His present having been made, the brave merely grunted and walked away, never to be heard from again; no trace of his name remains" (Herff 1973, 15). The girl was taken in by Julie Herf, and "years later made a happy marriage with Hermann Spiess," the Fortier organizer who succeeded Meusebach as commissioner general of the Adelsverein and who remained Herff's business partner (Herff 1973, 15; Figure 13).

The story was first published, in German, in Weber's early chronicle of Texas German pioneers (1894, part 1, pages 30–31). Weber collected oral history from former Fortiers, probably including Ferdinand Herff himself, and other Herff family members (Weber 1894, part 1, pages 8, 11-12). His version differs in some details from later renditions. It merits translation in full:

> Dr. Herff enjoyed the grand reputation of a "medicine man" with the Redskins and was princeps et carissimus [first and most dearly beloved] among the number of our civilizers. The Indian's virtue in showing recognition for a received favor, to the point of even forgetting his innate hatred toward the whites, may be effectively illustrated by the following episode. The physician had carried out a successful eye operation on a Comanche and in appreciation the grateful Indian promised him the gift of a young girl. All who were witness to this curious promise laughed and nobody took it seriously. Six months had passed when the healed Indian appeared at the settlement and delivered a small Mexican girl with the apology that "he had not been able to get hold of one earlier" and disappeared.[1] There can be no doubt that he had simply killed the parents of the child if they offered any resistance to the capture and thereby had committed a double crime, merely to show his gratitude. After one fruitless attempt to escape, the little one remained temporarily under the care of Fräulein Herf and later became the wife of Hermann Spiess. Their sons now live in Missouri. (Weber 1894, part 1, 30–31, translated by Wickham)

Figure 13. Hermann and Lena Spiess. Courtesy New Braunfels Herald-Zeitung.

Though it is hardly known, Herff also published his own reference to the surgery episode in a German newspaper, the *Allgemeine Auswanderungs-Zeitung* in 1848. His reference is included in a nine-part report about the Darmstadt Colony that is largely a treatise on immigrating to America, with some accounting of the Forty's migration as far as New Braunfels only. It was during their time in New Braunfels, waiting to depart for Bettina, that the Forty first met Comanches, those visiting under Santa Anna to receive presents promised in the Meusebach Treaty. Along with descriptions of Comanche riding and shooting prowess and singing, Herff gives the personal names of several of the Comanches. Among these is Kevamoi, the group's medicine man.[2] Herff then relates:

> The doctor of the tribe, who to begin with—just like the old colleagues
> in Europe—seemed to resent how young I was, sought help from me
> for his cataracts. With an imposing gesture I predicted blindness in six
> months, but told him that I would then give him back the light of his
> eyes, which seemed to comfort him, and, more generous than Santa
> Anna had been, he promised an honorarium consisting of 2 mules and
> a "zart mechicano hueipcha" (beautiful Mexican woman). (Herff 1848:44,
> column 691; translated by Wickham)

This passage is interesting because it establishes that the surgery
was arranged in New Braunfels, not in Bettina, as implied in the usual
version of the story. The patient is identified by name. It is also implied
that the patient's offer of remuneration was first made at this time, not
after the operation was completed. The payment here includes livestock
as well as a captive for a wife (Herff's Comanche is quite accurate:
"tsaatu mekhikano waiʔiʔipu," "good/fine/pretty Mexican woman").
At the same time, Herff's account does not confirm that the surgery
was done, at Bettina or anywhere else. Nor does it reveal whether the
Germans acquired a captive because of this transaction, or if the captive
was named Lena.

There is, however, an alternative story about the origin of Lena (or
Lina) Spiess. It originates in the unpublished papers of Hermann Spiess
and has been repeated without citation in the *Handbook of Texas* article
on Lena (Spiess Papers, 55–56, 60–64; Ragsdale 2010). Elements of the
story, with some variation, were also published in a 1968 New Braunfels
newspaper article about a visit to the town by Spiess's grandson Walter
Spiess ("Early Leader" 1968). Spiess's papers, as assembled by his
descendants in Missouri (where he and his wife settled upon leaving

Texas in 1867), contain three differing documents concerning Lena's origins. The first of these is a description of Lena's funeral on January 3, 1914, held at her final residence in Tropico, California, a Los Angeles suburb. It includes the following profile:

> Rev. Alton in the funeral address referred briefly to the touching and romantic history of the aged woman in whos (*sic*) memory they had assembled. Mrs. Spiess was rescued from a band of Indians down near the Rio Grande River when she was a very small child, so young that she was unable to give her rescuers anything of her parentage or her history. She could not even tell them her name, and hence her true name was never known.
>
> Her husband, Hermann Spiess was a member of the German settlement at New Braunfels. One day a band of Indians pitched camp near the settlement. The settlers observed that the Indians had this well dressed little child who manifestly was not their kind and had evidently been stolen. The settlers obtained possession of the little girl and she was placed in a Catholic Convent nearby, where she was cared for and educated. Hermann Spiess, who afterward became her husband, was one of the active participants in getting her from the Indians. (Spiess Papers, 55–56)

This profile appears to draw upon Lena's own memories of her origins as told to her descendants, but since it was evidently composed by the descendants or someone else, who had no first-hand knowledge of the Texas frontier, some of its details are questionable. The location of the rescue "down near the Rio Grande River" makes sense, but only from the perspective of a Missourian or Californian. A rescue at

New Braunfels is not impossible, but one at Bettina is at least as likely; remote descendants could well have been ignorant of the brief Bettina experiment and just assumed that New Braunfels was the site of all the activity. As for the convent element, a Catholic parish with chapel and school was established in New Braunfels in 1847, and Conventual Franciscan friars arrived in 1852, but nuns arrived only in 1868 (Haas 1968, 108, 110); "convent" could refer to the friar's facility.

Also found in the Spiess papers is an unsigned essay entitled "The Exile," a cloying biography of Lena Spiess written when she lived in Tropico (Spiess Papers, 59-64). The author acknowledges Lena as the source of some of the recollections and shows familiarity with the Darmstadter enterprise by naming Herff, Schleicher, Vogt, and Kriewitz among frontier heroes. In this story, a company of [German] pioneers come upon Comanches carrying two captive children, a "bright American boy" who the Indians will not part with, and the "frail weeping Mexican [girl] child" with whom they "readily dispensed." The girl is put in the care of an unnamed housekeeper in the home of Austrian Count Corith [Ernst Coreth] near New Braunfels, where among other things she witnesses a festive reception for Ferdinand Herff, returning from Germany with his bride. Here also she is tutored in German and English by Augusta and Minchen Schleicher. The girl then goes to live with Herman[n] Spiess and his sister Louise at their place on Waco Creek at [north of] New Braunfels; she is adopted with the name "Lena Spiess" and addresses Hermann as uncle. When Louise Spiess returns to Germany, Lena then moves to an orphanage run by Prof. Erfenberch [Ervendberg] and his wife. Then, as she attains womanhood, Lena marries Hermann Spiess and returns to Waco Springs. The bio concludes with passages describing some of Lena's faint pre-abduction memories and her longings for parents unknown, the growth of her family with Hermann, and relocations to Missouri and California.[3]

These two unpublished accounts of Lena Spiess's origins conform in some interesting ways to the recollections of Ferdinand Lindheimer, penned between 1876 and 1879:

> For a hand vise and a few files the Darmstadt colony negotiated for a still very young Mexican girl, who was handed over to my wife for supervision. She escaped from us several times, but was repeatedly captured and I scolded her: "titschi teiwo!" naughty girl. Mr. Hermann Spieß later had the child raised here in New Braunfels and she has now been his spouse for thirty years. (Lindheimer 1879, 69, trans. by Wickham; cf. Williams 2020, 114)

Lindheimer precedes this anecdote with another one, which not only illustrates the tenor of German-Comanche relations when it came to captives, but proves significant in establishing some chronology of the captive accounts:

> My two-year old (sic) son Eugen was a lively child who liked to walk naked in the open air. Santa Anna took a special liking to the child and offered me two beautiful mules and a young Mexican woman for the boy, who of course was not for sale. (Lindheimer 1879, 69; Williams 2020, 114)

Lindheimer's memory rings true if only for his accurate use of the Comanche language. Although translator John E. Williams laments that Lindheimer does not specify which Darmstadt colony is involved (Williams 2020, 114, n. 59), the only settlement referred to consistently in contemporary sources as the Darmstadt "colony" was the one at Bettina. Lindheimer's reference to "later . . . here in New Braunfels" indicates a contrast with the frontier outpost.

Lindheimer's account is a lynchpin of sorts because, in addition to fixing the location, it allows an approximate date to be assigned to the episodes he describes. Lindheimer's itinerary for gathering plant specimens can be retroactively constructed from the published record of his collections (Engelmann and Gray 1845; Gray 1850; Blankinship 1907), and thus his location at various places in Texas can be plotted month by month. This schedule shows that he was able to take advantage of Bettina as a base of operations during two intervals: when the colonists arrived in late September 1847 and into the ensuing winter, and again in July and August 1848, not long before the settlement was totally abandoned. We know from another contemporary source that during the first interval Lindheimer stayed at Bettina for one month, essentially October 1847 (Lindheimer 1848, column 778; Heinemann 1994, 319). His reference to son Eugen then comes into play. Max Eugen was born on February 5, 1847 (Goyne 1991, 6). He would have been only eight months old during Lindheimer's first stint at Bettina—not quite a toddler. But he would have been eighteen months old in August 1848, reasonably remembered later as a "two-year old" who was able to walk about. Therefore, unless Lindheimer met Santa Anna somewhere else, and no such event is found in the documentary record, Lindheimer heard the chief's offer for his son at Bettina in late summer 1848. The captive exchange Lindheimer writes about had to have taken place at Bettina either at that same time, or during fall 1847.

With this sequencing in mind, we return once more to Spiess's papers for the most significant of the three captive references found there (Spiess Papers, 115–17). Among his documents is a list of questions meant to elicit information about the origin of a "Mexican girl, rescued from the Comanche Indians, who is looking for her parents." The girl is presumably his wife Lena. It appears Spiess drafted this list so someone else he knew could inquire while in Mexico whether anyone remembered the girl or shared her memories of her origin place and relatives. The memories include details about the appearance of the girl's parents, her siblings and neighbor children, and her home and nearest town. These memories are more specific than most of those described in the dreamy prose of "The Exile," but the two accounts are not inconsistent. At the end of the list is an instruction to the intended solicitor: "Try your best with these details. It will be advisable not to mention me at all. Clergymen will surely find out who the parents were" (Spiess Papers, 116). It is not indicated that the questionnaire was ever put to use, but it may have been, since "The Exile" explains that when Lena came to yearn for knowledge of her parents, "[t]he kind husband would gladly have gratified her heart's desire, but with the meager evidence the search was fruitless" (Spiess Papers, 63). Most importantly, the list begins by explaining that "[i]n August 1848 the Comanche Indians brought a little Mexican girl to the settlements on the Llano in Texas. A German bought the girl from the Indians."

Some negative evidence reinforces the notion that Lena's rescue occurred in August 1848 rather than fall 1847, the other period when a Comanche visit to Bettina was documented. Two Bettina residents recorded the visit by a large party of Comanches in early November 1847. Reinhardt lists several tribes whose members visited the colony during its short existence, including a "big crowd" of Comanches led by Santa Anna that "camped only a short distance from us" and "staid some time" (Reinhardt 1899, 38). Schenck also describes what must have been the same Comanche visit, counting some 100 warriors plus wives and children, who had just recently left when he wrote his letter to his mother on November 11, 1847 (Hertzberg and Schenck 1988, 162–63). During this visit Santa Anna sent some men from his band in pursuit of some Wacos who had robbed Reinhardt earlier, and he tutored Schenck in Comanche star lore. And the resourceful and technically savvy Germans amazed the Indians by turning a new screw on their lathe to repair an Indian rifle. All of this took place roughly three months after Herff negotiated to perform his Indian surgery, lending some credence to the family story that he received a captive at this time. And the scenario of a captive exchange at this time becomes especially appealing if one chooses to read the obscure vertical date written on Friedrich's Drawing 1 as November 1847. But there is no evidence that the Comanches who gathered at Bettina that month brought a captive. Neither Reinhardt nor Schenck mention a captive, and if one had been presented in such a showy fashion as Friedrich's pictures indicate, it would be a strange omission given their other interesting details about the visit, although it is possible that they just quickly became inured to the captive business. As for why these same writers did not record an August 1848 redemption, it is reasonable to assume that whereas they were enthusiastic in sharing reports and memories of their early Indian encounters, they were much less motivated to discuss the final days of the settlement. Indeed, it is questionable if either Reinhardt or Schenck were still present there at such a late date. Reinhardt's absence at least is suggested by his comments that "[a]fter January 1848, no more Indians came" and "[i]n the summer of 1848, our colony . . . went to pieces . . . ." (Reinhardt 1899, 39).

When arrayed together and weighed in terms of their immediacy, these disparate accounts are not incompatible. They establish probable circumstances that can be summarized as follows. The Germans had other interactions with Comanches concerning captives in addition to the captive presentations at the Meusebach Treaty council recorded by Roemer and the anonymous officers. Santa Anna was involved in all of these additional episodes. One of these interactions involved Ferdinand Herff. Herff made the arrangements for his celebrated surgery, with curious payment tendered, while still in New Braunfels; in all likelihood he undertook the operation some weeks later at Bettina. He may have received a captive as payment for his medical services. If he did, her delivery could have coincided with the November 1847 Comanche visit, although her delivery has been described as a casual, individual gesture by the grateful patient, not part of any large event. Nevertheless, it is not independently substantiated in primary written sources that this transfer actually took place, even though Reinhardt, Schenck, Lindheimer, and Herff himself, among others, were in a position as eyewitnesses to do so. The story of Herff's interaction with Kevamoi appears to have been conflated with the story of Lena Spiess. Lena was purchased, not received as a payment or gift. She was redeemed by Hermann Spiess and Ferdinand Lindheimer in some joint effort, perhaps including other Germans too. Unlike the putative Herff transaction, this one took place during the final days of the colony and clearly involved a group of Indian visitors. As Bettina dissolved, Lena was taken to New Braunfels and raised for the next three years in a series of foster situations involving several of the notable citizens of the German community there, ex-Fortiers and others. Her death notice indicates that she married Spiess in 1851, at about age fifteen (cf. Spiess Papers, 56; Ragsdale 2010).

It is tempting to wonder if the Mexican girl in the Herff or Spiess and Lindheimer accounts was the same one offered several months earlier at the Meusebach Treaty council. There is no documentary evidence to this effect. Incidentally, "two mules and a girl" seems to have been the standard Comanche offer for something else they valued, since both Herff and Lindheimer mention this specific price; either that, or Lindheimer had read Herff's 1848 account and, writing thirty years later, "remembered" this detail in his own experience.

CHAPTER ELEVEN
WHERE?

The related question of where the D1 and D2 event took place requires further excursions both literal and figurative. The first location possibility for the captive exchange in D1 and D2 is the site or vicinity of the Meusebach Treaty signing. A visit to this site on the anniversary date of March 2, 2021, revealed important similarities and differences between it and Friedrich's depiction. Fortunately, the purported exact site was marked with a large engraved stone during the 1936 Texas Centennial. It lies on the southeast side of FM 2732/Sloan Road 13.8 road miles southwest of the town of San Saba. This road follows the San Saba River upstream along its south bank for about seventeen miles before terminating about two miles east of the confluence of Brady Creek with the San Saba. The area today is rural, with intermittent ranches and pecan plantations and abundant open rangeland. Driving southwest along the road one sees several vistas that generally resemble the landscape in Friedrich's drawings 1 and 3. These consist essentially of level plain in the foreground and a ridge composed of multiple hills at an appreciable distance from the road. These vistas appear here and there on both sides of the road, as there is a ridge on each side of the river valley. At first glance, then, Friedrich's drawing could be looking either northwest or southeast. In the northwest views, however, the river inserts itself in the foreground, evident in the meandering line of majestic pecans and other hardwoods that rim its banks. Since there is no such river gallery in Friedrich's pictures, his view is more likely to the southeast, as the historical marker suggests (Figure 14).

Looking southeast over the property from the marker, one is struck immediately by two variances. First, at this spot in the valley the south bank ridge is relatively low and close to the river, and it rises abruptly as a mostly uniform mass covered in cedar. It does not present a series of open rolling hills rising at a distance and fading toward the horizon as in Friedrich's drawings. Secondly, the plain in the foreground spans only

Figure 14. The Meusebach Treaty site. Photo by Daniel J. Gelo.

about 400 feet from the road to the foot of the ridge, comprising twelve acres, barely enough to accommodate the busy scene that Friedrich rendered, and much of it is covered by a pond. This pond is fed by several springs at the foot of the ridge, most heavily from one that issues from the right background, collectively called Sloan Pool Spring. As a second nearby historical marker explains, this stream was impounded for a mill by the first permanent settlers, around 1857. The pond has given rise to a dense line of now-mature secondary tree growth on its sheltered southeast edge, along the ridge base. The dam and millrace are still evident in the left foreground of the site; from there the creek flows down to the river.

Despite these conspicuous differences, there are two obscure details in Friedrich's drawings which may summon this exact location. Toward the left center of D1, one saddled Indian horse stands with front legs splayed and mouth to the ground. Though it might appear that it is grazing with its split reins trailing on the ground, the two lines running leftward from its mouth could also suggest a stream of water, crossing the scene from back right to front left, from which the horse is drinking. This stream would correspond to the one at the treaty site, later submerged under its impoundment. Also, the actual stream carves a noticeable small escarpment or cut bank, facing left (northeast), where it flows out from the base of the hill toward the far right of the open ground (Figure 15). Friedrich took pains to draw a land feature like this in both of his captive exchange drawings; he indicates topographic relief in multiple ways: shading of the ground, dangling legs of some of the people reclining on the feature, and the perspective of nearby lines of Indians and Germans. In D1 the cut bank is prominent in the far right of the picture, with five Indians lounging on it and another standing. Though nothing like a stream is readily evident in D2, the bank appears again, right of center, with a dog, some lounging Indians, and others standing or mounted. It seems odd that the artist would reproduce these details twice unless he had some actual land feature in mind. Along with these two landscape details, the foreground animals correspond in a general way to the skins that the Indians offered for trade at the parlay, as reported by Roemer (1849, 323; 1983, 268).

This interpretation is speculative and assumes that the captive presentation was conducted at the same spot as the treaty council, and that the council site was accurately marked in 1936. One or both events might have been held instead at another similar spot nearby. The

Figure 15. Close-up of cut bank at Meusebach Treaty site. Photo by Daniel J. Gelo.

match between the cut bank in the drawings and one discernible on the grounds today, which is less prominent than the one in the pictures, could be purely coincidental. (A potentially similar topographic feature, another bank, this one triangular—though perhaps it is a notch, depending on how one judges the vertical hatching—is carefully drawn into the wooded ridgeline below the horizon of D1, and something vaguely like it, a gap on the horizon, appears in a comparable position in D2, but nothing like this feature is noticeable at the actual site, at least with today's vegetation.) The most that can be said with certainty is that the springs and sheltering ridges would have made for a very attractive meeting place, and the pecan groves in the wider curves of the river nearby would have been ideal campsites from the Comanche viewpoint.

A later artistic representation of the treaty council grounds, of which there are two versions, offers some instructive comparisons with Friedrich's drawings. The primary version is an oil painted in 1927 by Lucy Meusebach Marschall (Mrs. Ernest Marschall, daughter of John Meusebach; 1865–1961) which hangs in the Vereinskirche Museum in Fredericksburg (Figure 16). Marschall's painting shows John Meusebach and twenty Comanche men sitting around a council fire on buffalo hides beneath two towering oaks. The trees look like ones present at the edge of the site today. Encircling the negotiators at a distance and looking on are more Germans and Indians, a Mexican with sombrero, attendant horses, and further still, tipis. While the background ridge is green and immediate, like the one seen toward the southeast at the marked site today, its relatively rugged ridgeline with a pronounced point on the left better resembles the view toward the northwest, though no river is evident. The foreground plain is grand

and fades off into a distant haze toward the right in a manner worthy of Alfred Jacob Miller or the Hudson River School (or Hermann Lungkwitz).

The more commonly seen version of this image is a simplistic copy of the center section of the Marschall painting produced around 1947 by an unnamed artist for the Meusebach Treaty centennial celebration, with nineteen instead of twenty Indian councilors and more sombreros (Figure 17; King 1967, 64). Both Friedrich's works and the Marschall painting and its facsimile depend on a kind of modular composition (standardized details of dress to distinguish ethnicities; figures repeated and assembled in discrete groupings) and certain exaggerations of scale for theatrical effect, and in this way they resemble each other even though their subjects, methods, and details are quite different.

Another more recent painting of the treaty grounds also merits consideration, this a six-by-eight-foot oil on canvas by contemporary

Figure 16. *Meusebach-Comanche Indian Treaty* by Lucy Meusebach Marschall (1927). Courtesy Pioneer Museum, Fredericksburg, TX. Photo by Daniel J. Gelo.

Figure 17. Painting of Meusebach Treaty council after Marschall 1927, anonymous (circa 1947).

Hill Country muralist Lee Casbeer installed in 2016 in the now-closed Treaty House Cocktail Lounge and Wine Bar in Fredericksburg (Lowry 2019; Figure 18). Casbeer depicts a small circle of Germans and Indians, with Santa Anna handing Meusebach a peace pipe and Buffalo Hump standing nearby; the group is framed by two large trees, and further out there is a sampling of the spectators and tipis presented in the Marschall painting.

His central figures strongly resemble *Lasting Friendship*, a heroic-sized bronze sculpture group showing the peace pipe exchange by J. (Jay) Hester that was unveiled in the Fredericksburg Marktplatz in 1997 to commemorate the 150th anniversary of German-Comanche concord (Figure 19). In the background is a finely rendered landscape with an extensive plain bounded by a ridge only partly clothed in cedar. The ridge looks very much like the one on the northwest side

Figure 18. *Treaty with the Comanches, 1847* by Lee Casbeer. Courtesy of the artist.

of the river. On the far side of the plain is a substantial body of water that could represent either the spring pond at the actual site (though such a pond probably did not exist before 1857), or else the San Saba River (though devoid of trees). Casbeer trained in Italy, and his mural displays sophisticated, realistic treatment of human anatomy and landscape. Like its predecessors, however, the Casbeer mural strays from an exacting depiction of the treaty site while capturing some of its appearance. For this reason, the treaty paintings do not provide a precise match to Friedrich's scene or confirm its precise location. They remain highly relevant, however, because along with Friedrich's drawings they constitute a diachronic corpus that catalogs repeatable visual elements which, separately or in combination, have become evocative of the foundational saga.

Some nagging questions cast doubt on the proposition that Friedrich intended to draw the treaty site, or the captive transaction said to have occurred there. The Germans conducted their journey on horseback, yet none of the horses shown in D1 and D2 are clearly associated with the Germans. Accounts of the treaty council mention numerous Comanche tipis ("tents" or "wigwams") in the vicinity, and the three later pictures of the event include tipis in the background, but no tipis were drawn by Friedrich. (One answer to this objection is that the tipis are behind the viewer, in a bend right along the edge of the woods lining the river as described by participants [Penniger 1896, 92–93; 1971, 40; 2020, 127; Roemer 1849, 320–21; 1983, 266], and therefore Friedrich's picture is more accurate than those of his successors). Also,

Figure 19. *Lasting Friendship* bronze sculpture group by J. Hester (1997), Fredericksburg, TX Marktplatz. Photo by C. B. "Hoppy" Hopkins.

Friedrich was not yet in Texas when the treaty council occurred, and it could be argued he was more likely to have drawn a later event that he actually witnessed. Julie Herf, shown as an onlooker in D1, was not there either; the treaty expedition included no women. The large stone wall in D1 is another detail that could not have been at the treaty scene.

Some of these questions and anachronisms seem to go away if a different location is considered. An alternative possibility is that Friedrich's setting for D1 and D2 was the Bettina settlement, and the event referenced is the captive redemption described in the Herff or Lindheimer and Spiess stories. The first persuasive point of argument is that Friedrich would have been more likely to draw an event he actually attended, and he definitely lived at Bettina. Julie Herf also resided there, so her presence in D1 suggests Bettina. We do not know that dogs were present at the treaty site, but we do know there were several at the commune. This location might also account for the stone wall pictured in D1. And the landscape Friedrich drew might resemble the relatively open and gently rising terrain looking north from the Llano River. Most importantly, two Bettina residents recorded a visit there by a large party of Comanches in early November 1847, and Spiess recorded another visit to "the Llano settlements" in August 1848. According to her obituary, Lena Spiess was a "well-dressed little child" when found by the Germans, much like the captive Friedrich drew (Spiess Papers, 56).

Led by accomplished local historian Glenn Hadeler, the authors visited the place where Bettina once stood on July 30, 2021. The site lies about two miles east of Castell on the north side of the Llano River, west of the Elm Creek confluence, on private property. The creek runs toward the old Bettina tract from the northwest with little sinuosity before forming four bends, the last turning almost due south to join the river. It flows today only after heavy rains and was dry when we viewed it. Its bed is deep and wide, with abrupt banks; it is uniformly filled with sandy silt, devoid of visible boulders except below a low-water crossing where scouring has exposed bedrock, and lined with tall trees and bushes. The stream bisects the low flat ridge that runs parallel to the river, producing two distinct sections of elevated ground, one to the south and west, and a slightly higher section to the north and east. The commune site appears as a remnant clearing on the relatively level top of the southerly ridge section, bounded by the last creek bends. Here, as elsewhere in the area, the soil is pale tan and sandy; we observed topsoil depth of one foot or more at an excavation further west on the same ridge. Large patches of sandstone bedrock are exposed in some spots, and gleaming chunks of quartzite are abundantly scattered on the surface. The area is otherwise covered in open bunchgrass, overgrown in places by brush consisting mainly of mesquite, persimmon, yucca, prickly pear, lechuguilla, and tasajillo. A few large and stately oaks not unlike the tree in Friedrich's Drawing 2 grow on the edges of the remnant clearing, and as one moves north and east toward the creek a tall dense gallery of mixed hardwoods is encountered. Hadeler observed that the brush in the former clearing had increased dramatically in the last twenty-five years. Cow paths allow passage around the site. Evidence of the former settlement is limited to a few worked or arranged stones on the ground surface, plus some foundation or footing stones that have been exposed by an animal burrow. Some of the stones are local sandstone, while others, including the foundation stones and one large nicely squared block, are limestone, which is not native to the immediate area (Figure 20).

Some effort was made to visualize the earlier appearance of the commune landscape and the views that were afforded from the site. In pre-settlement times periodic fires ignited by lightning or Indians would have burned off the brush and maintained a vegetation regime with grasses and only occasional mesquites and oaks (e.g., Hertzberg and Schenck 1988, 156). The severe drought under way from 1845 into the 1860s would also have limited plant growth (see Herff 1848:40, column 630; Lindheimer 1848, column 778; Winfrey and Day 1995, 141; Hämäläinen 2008, 296). The settlers would have maintained or enhanced these open conditions. Especially with reduced tree growth, local elevation differences, which are negligible in absolute terms, would be more apparent. With such allowances, something like the contrast between riverine prairie and lateral upland that Lindheimer noted at

Figure 20. Worked stone at the Bettina site. Photo by C. B. "Hoppy" Hopkins.

the time of settlement is recognizable: "Not far from the ford they found a patch of land suitable for cultivation, some prairie stretching along the Llano with light soil and dotted with mesquite trees, which is always a sign of fertile land. The nearby higher ground parallel to the river was wooded with oaks (post oak and live oak)" (Lindheimer 1848, column 777). Also sensible is the appreciable slope of the land southward well across the river, so that House Mountain and neighboring high points are clearly visible from the vicinity of the commune site, as suggested in one account (Lindheimer 1848, column 778). And looking north and eastward from the commune site across the creek to the slightly higher segment of the plateau, and imagining this view without the current tall trees, there are elevations, contours, and a horizon line very much like those drawn by Friedrich in his captive pictures (Figure 21).

Figure 21. View north from Bettina commune site toward higher ground. Photo by Daniel J. Gelo.

It seems likely then that the Bettina site was one of the settings, if not the principal one, for Friedrich's captive drawings. His backgrounds correspond to the landscape looking north from the place where remains of the settlement buildings are found, or else a spot somewhat further to the east. The view is to the north, and encompasses the ridge beyond the creek, with the creek cutting through from left background to right foreground, though not obviously. In this view, the cut bank on which spectators are posed is the east bank of Elm Creek (Figure 22). The Germans and Indians gathered for their meeting at or close by the settlement and the captive was presented there.

Even with imaginative adjustments, however, Friedrich's drawings cannot be said to furnish an undeniably precise recreation of the Bettina setting. For one thing, the stone wall that seems to suggest the inroads of civilization is not likely to have existed at Bettina so soon after the settlers' arrival, if ever. Colonists' accounts of Bettina mention buildings and cleared fields, but not walls or fences (though the settlers of nearby Castell immediately formed a squad to build fences there, according to Wilhelm Hermes [Haas 1968, 41]). They would have had to build some fencing, but in the early years, settlers depended on wood rail fencing, and stone fence building only became common after the late 1850s (see Bracht 1931, 136–37; Newcomb and Carnahan 1978, 84, 150, 178; Jordan 1966, 164-65). The tall German stone fences were built with flat rocks continually gathered from plowed fields and took a long time to build. They were enduring structures, and those built in the Hill County are still standing. Yet no stone wall or fence, or the definite remains of one, have ever been noted at the Bettina site.

How else to explain the building stones found around the site? As far as we know, the commune structures ultimately included: a large

Figure 22. Author team comparing drawings with east bank of Elm Creek. July 30, 2021. Photo by Christopher J. Wickham.

barracks building of log poles and beams covered with reeds; two small log cabins, one serving as a kitchen, and another for food storage; and two "fachwerk" (in this case, adobe) houses. The settlers built a small windmill to turn a hand-mill, to grind corn (Lindheimer 1848, 778–79; Reinhardt 1899, 37–38). There is no indication that they dug a well, and it appears they simply carried water up from the river. They may have built a cistern near their dwellings, but none is recorded. In one of the adobe houses was "a fire place 12 feet broad and built of rock" (Reinhardt 1899, 38). The stones found today could have been parts of several of the known structures, though it has long been supposed that at least some were from the large fireplace: "Today only the sad remains of a dilapidated chimney mark the spot where 47 years ago the first settlement was founded in 'Vereinsland'" (Weber 1894, part 1, page 28; cf. Baird 2010, 25).

Also, the armed Germans in D1 and D2—nearly every man carries a rifle—do not fit well with the Bettina setting. The Meusebach expedition members were well armed, at first brandishing their guns and telling the Penatekas they would use them if necessary, then discharging them in a show of trust (Penniger 1896, 92; 1971, 39; 2020, 127; King 1967, 115). During the first night that the Forty occupied their commune site, "everyone sat around the table with their double-barreled rifles in their hands" (Lindheimer 1848, column 778, translated by Wickham), but fears soon faded, and the Germans would not have had much reason to carry their guns during a peaceful gathering several months after the settlement was established. Almost as questionable in a commune scene are Julie Herf's elegant attire and the formal, uniform dress of the German men. Unfortunately, there are no other images of the Bettina settlement comparable to those of the Meusebach Treaty council which would support further speculation on the details of Friedrich's drawings.

Other questions pertain to the captive exchange itself. As previously demonstrated, there is no evidence that the Comanches who gathered at Bettina in November 1847 brought a captive. Neither Reinhardt nor Schenck mention one. The Herff legend does tell of a captive at Bettina, but this story is not substantiated by other observers. The legend relates that the captive in this case was dropped off casually by Herff's patient, who we find was a medicine man, and not presented by a headman before large numbers of Comanches and Germans in an open landscape, as drawn by Friedrich. Is it simply the case that Friedrich, in drawing many Indians, delivers a more accurate account of this episode than Herff family lore? This is possible, but it is unlikely that a contrary legend would have been passed down along with the pictures in the same family. These objections leave the August 1848 Comanche visit to Bettina or a neighboring settlement on the Llano during which Lena Spiess was redeemed as the more likely subject of Friedrich's work. Even so, his drawings include large numbers of Indians and Germans not directly attested to in accounts of Lena's redemption, and a dramatic landscape that is not so readily recognizable when the site is reconnoitered.

It is alternately possible that Friedrich was exacting and drew an event in D1 and D2 that is not recorded anywhere else. If so, his pictures would be especially valuable for expanding on the German-Comanche legacy. It seems implausible, however, that an event of the scope portrayed by Friedrich would not have been recorded along with the other captive presentations in published memoirs and oral tradition.

In any case, it is significant that, while several photos exist of redeemed Comanche captives (e.g., Corwin 1959; Zesch 2004), Friedrich's drawings are the only known period images of a Comanche captive made while the person was in captivity.

CHAPTER TWELVE
Conclusions

The remaining vagaries lead us toward a new premise, that Friedrich's D1 and D2 are not exact depictions of a single place or event, but rather creative composites with commemorative intention. They could be hybrids of the Meusebach Treaty and Bettina locations and events, or others, all with a healthy measure of artistic license. Remarkably, both the treaty grounds and Bettina contain analogs to some of the distinctive landscape details that the artist made sure to repeat from one drawing to the other, and therefore neither site is easily privileged as the source of Friedrich's mental imagery. To the extent that he was recreating the treaty setting, it seems that like subsequent artists Friedrich sought to capture the general look of the place but did not attempt to recreate it exactly, instead drawing upon imagery from the area while taking liberties with the scale and appearance of the natural features, to give himself enough space to relate his narrative. It does appear that he was familiar with the look of the San Saba valley, which lies less than twenty miles north-northwest of the Llano County property that he acquired in 1848. On the other hand, it does not seem that Friedrich would have had much if any opportunity to explore the treaty site around the time D1 was likely made, busy as he was with the dissolution of the Bettina colony. If instead, as seems likely, Friedrich was using Bettina as his main reference, his pictures again could have evoked the location without being exact reproductions. In similar fashion, the main action of the captive scene could be historically authentic but not necessarily or primarily a singular historical fact. It follows then that the D3 wagon train scene is of a similar nature. Here Friedrich did depict a single event, at a single or composite place, and he likely took part in the ride, but would not have looked down upon the procession from the Indians' vantage. In their contrived (but not deceptive) quality the three drawings might be called "artistic historical fiction." Friedrich's purpose was not photographic, but didactic and memorial.

Under this hypothesis, the drawing details do the work of adding realism and ensuring that the three drawings would be clearly connected in posterity. Friedrich makes the effort to depict the landscape the same way in both captive presentation pictures, with at least one diagnostic detail, the scarp on the right where some Indians are lounging. Other specific repeated details include the two jaguars, the German men with tucked pants, the way the chief holds the captive, and the Indian with lance and quiver standing with his back turned to the viewer. Some details, such as men carrying slain deer and the German making an announcement, are included in D2 but not D1. Some other details are dubious and demonstrate that Friedrich was not drawing from life. These would include the animals laid out for an idyllic feast, the idealized poses of several figures in D1, and the stereotypic headbands, quivers, and the trailer warbonnets. The bonnets are most interesting because Friedrich confirms their early existence on the Southern Plains, a significant ethnologic fact, yet employs them in what is probably a fictitious manner to underscore the Indian leaders' identities, contrary to eyewitness reports, at least those from the Meusebach Treaty council.

It seems overly generous to compare Friedrich's sketches with masterpieces of western American art, yet in their conceptualization, Friedrich's D1 and D2 are not unlike Frederic Remington's 1903 oil *Fight for the Water Hole* (Neff 2000, 80–85). Remington used accounts of the famous 1874 Buffalo Wallow Fight in the Texas panhandle as the basis for an otherwise imaginary scene of combat between cowboys and Indians in the stark Arizona desert. Remington's evocative power derives from the superiority of his coloration and lighting, and only secondarily, if at all, by summoning viewers' knowledge of an actual event. Friedrich conjures artistic effect in the opposite way, relying on viewers' familiarity with events, and a few stereotypic visual cues, much more than artistic technique. But both artists end up with works that at once distill and transcend literal history.

To do so, Friedrich produced his art sometime after the events portrayed, probably soon after, and with some purposeful sequencing. It is first worth reaffirming the opinion that all three drawings were done by the same person, and that the person was Wilhelm Friedrich. Casual comparison of D1 and D2 might raise questions about the consistency of technique, but the differences are explainable when D1 is viewed as a more careful reproduction of D2 by the same hand, in pencil rather than ink. Likewise, the rendition of Friedrich's name is different on D3 from D1, and each of these is quite different from Friedrich's elegant script signature as found on numerous real estate documents, but these differences arguably result from different writing instruments and context-driven style choices (and in D3, the possibility that a different person re-wrote the torn legend).

Different production sequences could be posited for the drawings depending on how the obscure dates on the front of D1 and D2 are read and whether the dates on D1 and D3 verso are accepted as accurate, although the firm dates of the Meusebach captive presentations and Lena Spiess redemption, along with attention to the artist's compositional choices, point to only a couple of alternate, parsimonious explanations. In the first option, which accepts the possibility that the Meusebach Treaty captive was Friedrich's subject, D2 was drawn in 1847 or 1849, and D1 was drawn in the same time frame. In the second scenario, favoring Lena Spiess as the inspiration, both captive drawings were made in 1849. In either case, D2 was done first. In it the artist is concerned with displaying the entire scene, and the captive exchange is one element of that scene, noticeable but not centered. The pen work has an impromptu feel. Drawing 1 was done later, as an attempt to restate and refine the same scene, working from D2, but this time with a light pencil, more care, and more of a focus on the captive exchange element. By shifting his viewpoint to the left in this version, Friedrich places the captive in the center of the composition and provides careful framing of the main action from both right and left. A curious effect of this shift is that the semi-circle of surrounding mounted warriors which is implied but not fully depicted in D2 is "completed" on its left side in D1, so that a full view of these warriors is furnished only when the two drawings are viewed together; they become complementary. Along with this shift, Friedrich also eliminates obvious indication that the captive is struggling, yielding a more benign image of the captive presentation, one more compatible with positive memories of the interaction. It is almost as if in the time elapsed since D2 was made, the Germans found the Comanches less dangerous than earlier thought. In D1 greater effort is devoted to detailing the captive's dress, hat crowns, pockets, weaponry, headbands, and pelage of the animals. Most instrumental is the inclusion of the man explaining the event to Julie Herf, for just as he does so, Friedrich explains the German-Comanche relationship to all of us. These characteristics of D1 along with its written labels along the bottom amount to greater care and precision, and a more authoritative presentation of the captive exchange narrative. Drawing 3 was also done in the more careful style and was probably made in 1848 as the front and back of the picture indicate. If D3 is indeed the earliest of the three pictures, then it appears that D1 was drawn in the same style to compose a matched set, just as the two drawings have been handed down.

For whom did Friedrich make his sketches? He may have drawn them purely for his own satisfaction. Or, since they were owned by the Herffs, it may be that this family was his intended audience. Theirs was a close-knit family, proud of its German heritage and pioneer status, highly cultured, and to a person determined to make a positive mark on society. Their family tree and three-generation memoir (Herff 1978) leave little doubt that the senior Herffs were keen to preserve their legacy for their descendants and the public, and Friedrich's drawings also served this intention well. We know too that Friedrich and Ferdinand Herff continued to participate in a community of former Fortiers and their associates long after the dissolution of Bettina. Men like Louis Reinhardt, Friedrich Schenck, Adam Vogt, and Emil Kriewitz would have appreciated Friedrich's efforts to honor their common experience on the early frontier. And regardless of their historical accuracy, the captive presentation drawings would have had added emotional resonance for Herff and others in his circle because of their personal experiences with the exchange of one or more Mexican captive girls. To the extent that Friedrich's drawings were understood to depict Lena Spiess, it could be that their ownership by the Herff family led to or reinforced the conflation of Lena's story with the tale of Ferdinand's surgery. For those colonists with upper-class origins there was no firm divide between the old and new worlds in the early days. Several returned to Germany around 1850 for good, or came back to live out their days in Texas. Through these connections, Friedrich's audience could well have extended to the home country, and more of his sketches may exist there. His drawings correlate with the many rich letters that the settlers sent to their relatives in Germany (e.g., Lauckhard 1931; Hertzberg and Schenck 1988; Fey 1994, 157–94; Wurster 2008; Gelo and Wickham 2018, 114–115).[1]

In addition to satisfying these kinds of immediate objectives, Friedrich developed a novel approach to representing the pioneer experience: by focusing on cultural interaction, turning it into the Indian-pioneer experience. This move is most evident in D3, which privileges the Indian viewpoint on the very arrival of the German settlers. This drawing stands in contrast, for example, to Catlin's illustration of the dragoons meeting the Comanches, rendered from the dragoon's viewpoint, and more so with Leutze's wagon train painting, which is totally absorbed in the ambitions and travails of the settlers, with no Indians visible. Even considering that some of Friedrich's immediate audience members were cultivated, he was forcing his original viewers, and continues to force us, to adopt an unexpected perspective. Drawings 1 and 2 evince a more measured version of this approach, in which the scene is not constructed from the Indian viewpoint, but rather from an anonymous, external vantage, with the Indians prominent and equivalent to the Germans as subjects. Friedrich's manipulation of perspective by showing human figures from the back calls to mind the work of his namesake Caspar David Friedrich (1774–1840; no known relation to Wilhelm), the most prominent exponent of German Romantic painting (Schmied 1975; Russo 1999).[2] Along with this experimentation in viewpoint, Friedrich establishes overall a rational rather than emotional connection between his viewers and the people and environment he depicts. These artistic achievements are very much in keeping with Friedrich's technical training and with the German colonists' commitment to objectivity and human rights.

On the face of it, Friedrich's drawings are representations of space (the Texas landscape) in space (his sheets of paper), yet they incorporate an intricate cross weave of time. The sketches tell a story and thus imply a timeline, a beginning, middle, and end. On one level, we can isolate in D1 and D2 the story of the captive girl, who started in her Mexican family, was removed to the Indian community, and is on the point of transitioning to the German group. The "now" of the drawing therefore also contains both the past of the captivity and the future of a new life. On another level, time is an essential component of this space because, from a wider perspective, D1 and D2 (also D3) mark the passing of one way of life to a new dominant order. Again, the past and the future are woven into the depicted moment. Furthermore, one could easily make a case for interpreting the captive as a metaphor for the space as it crosses over into a new time.

A person of Wilhelm Friedrich's interests and vision was likely to have some notion of the coming developments initiated by the Fortiers and their fellow German settlers. He lived to see the towns they founded or populated in and near the Fisher-Miller Grant—Fredericksburg,

Castell, Boerne, Comfort, Mason, Llano—become viable and at times prosperous communities. And by the early 1850s, Friedrich would have realized that however marvelous, the Meusebach peace would not protect the Penatekas from the onslaught of settlement. By 1855, most Penatekas had withdrawn toward the Colorado and Brazos headwaters, and one faction agreed to move onto a reservation nearly 200 miles north of Bettina, but facing continuing duress there, they were removed to Indian Territory, present southwest Oklahoma, in 1859. Friedrich probably would not, however, have predicted that a few of his sketches, meant to exercise his love of drawing and entertain and inform some friends, would expand knowledge of Comanche ethnology and the German–Indigenous experience, and secure his legacy as a significant figure in the history of Central Texas frontier settlement.

ENDNOTES

INTRODUCTION

[1] Charles was christened "Carl"; his middle name appears variously as Adelbert or Adam.

CHAPTER ONE

[1] As Scott Zesch has pointed out, the Germans' notion of intermarriage was one-sided. They expected to marry Indian women, but did not desire to see German women married to Indian men (Zesch 2004, 32).

CHAPTER TWO

[1] "It is nearly impossible today to determine who belonged to the *Darmstädters* originally" (Reichstein 2001, 41–42; cf. Heinemann 1994, 294–97). Nevertheless, with guidance from previous researchers and an independent reading of the relevant sources, it is possible to come to probable and definite conclusions about Wilhelm Friedrich's life and career in Texas. Sources pertinent to Friedrich's biography include: Weber 1894; Reinhardt 1899; Biesele 1930; Dielmann 1954; Haas 1968; Geue 1970; Geue and Geue 1972; Herff 1973; Hertzberg and Schenck 1988; Heinemann 1994; Lich 1996; Reichstein 2001; Morgenthaler 2007, 2014; Evans 2010; Adam-Hurst 2012; Boardman 2018; *https://de.wikipedia.org/wiki/Griedel*; Galveston Historical Foundation Immigration Database; Find a Grave online database; records of the Corps Starkenburgia fraternity and the Technical University of Darmstadt; and records of the Texas General Land Office. Co-author Moon had separately amassed information from primary documents on Friedrich's life course and role in the development of Boerne, Texas, some of which has been incorporated. Specific citations are given in the text where warranted.

2   The records were translated by Wickham. We are indebted to Frau Dr. Annegret
     Holtmann-Mares, Director of the University Archive, Technical University of
     Darmstadt, for locating the records for us and making them available.

3   The newspaper was edited by Dr. Heinrich Künzel, an instructor at the Darmstadt
     Vocational School and mentor to the Forty (see Heinemann 1994, 287, 298, 335).
     Künzel could be the "K." in Friedrich's grade reports. The declaration signed
     by Friedrich, Schenck, and Schleicher was considered important enough to be
     reprinted in the *Allgemeine Auswanderungs-Zeitung* under the headline "Die
     Darmstädter Texas-Gesellschaft" (Friedrich et al. 1847).

4   The original Darmstadt or Darmstaedter Farm was located on Comal Creek 2.5
     miles west of New Braunfels, on land purchased and occupied in summer 1847.
     Ferdinand Herff was explicit that this farm was built as a waystation while the
     Forty were still poised in New Braunfels, though another contemporary article
     attributed to Lindheimer (but probably composed by a Forty member) erroneously
     states that the farm was laid out only after Bettina was established (Herff 1848:43,
     column 674; Lindheimer 1848, columns 778–9; cf. Weber 1894, part 1, pages
     27–28; Hertzberg and Schenck 1988, 158–59). In late 1848 some immigrants
     staying at this farm started a second one 8 miles southwest of New Braunfels near
     present Danville, Texas (Weber 1894, part 1, pages 39–40). This second farm has
     also been referred to as the Darmstaedter Farm, leading to some confusion. Both
     settlements were sold off after about a year. The exact location of the farm structures
     has not been researched. See also Biesele 1930, 157, 168; Chabot 1937, 371; Geue
     1970, 20; Haas n.d., 1972, 6B; Reichstein 2001, 48.

5   Reichstein at one point designates Friedrich as a forester. This claim appears to
     be based on information about Friedrich's fraternity membership and is either an
     outright error or an allusion to Friedrich's coursework in science and drafting, some
     of which overlapped with the standard German prerequisites for forestry. Later
     Reichstein lists Friedrich as a lawyer, citing a list composed by Hermann Spiess
     when the group formed, which he implies is identical to the roster later published
     in the newspaper (Reichstein 2001, 21, 41–42; see also Lauckhard 1931, 96).

6   Several sources claim that the settlers named this new farm Tusculum after Cicero's
     country retreat. Tusculum was actually a hill city a comfortable distance from
     Rome where many patricians kept country villas. While the designation sounds
     appropriate for a community with classical aspirations, there is no contemporary
     evidence that the settlers gave the new location this or any other name. The claim
     ostensibly began with Biesele (1930, 172), who apparently misread Weber's
     comment that Ferdinand Herff "acquired a significant amount of real estate in

the immediate vicinity of the little town [Boerne] and there created for himself a friendly Tusculum," alluding to the doctor's country home (Weber 1894, part 2, page 9, translated by Wickham).

7   Friedrich was not shy in attempting to perpetuate the original spelling where possible in the early land surveys he conducted.

8   Few Texas German settlers supported slavery or secession, and some were vigorously opposed, but many remained loyal to their adopted state (see Biesele 1930, 195-207; 1995; Jordan 1966, 180, 182-85, 194; Buenger 1979; Goyne 1991, 186-87; Morgenthaler 2007, 135-37; Kearney 2010; Johnson 2020, 50-51).

9   The grim news somehow made it back to Friedrich's alma mater, for the Darmstadt Vocational School directory of former students for 1885 includes Friedrich, "powdermaker in Texas," deceased (Adressen-Verzeichnis 1885, 21, translated by Wickham). It was repeated in an 1890 chronicle of Friedrich's fraternity, though with an erroneous death date of January 1864 (Scharfenberg and Fabricius 1890, 137; cf. Weber 1894, part 1, page 34; Heinemann 1994, 337). Census and burial records from 1880 to 2021 provide for the following sequel, meticulously reconstructed by co-author Bryden Moon and drawing owner Bob Phelps. Friedrich's widow married M. L. Block, a bookkeeper of Australian birth, and she and her daughters moved with him to New Orleans. She had no children with her second husband. Daughter Charlotte remained unmarried and lived with her mother; daughter Alice married Henry Thurston Brown and had one son and two daughters. In 1886 Alice Block, again a widow, with her daughters and son-in-law sold Wilhelm Friedrich's Boerne property to developer David S. Irons. Alice Block was working as a housekeeper for another family in 1910, and died in July 1914. Both of her and Wilhelm Friedrich's daughters died in December 1929. Alice Brown's son Reuben had one son, Shelby Wood Brown, and one daughter, Marjorie F. Brown, who died respectively in 1957 and 1968. All of these family members rest in Greenwood Cemetery, New Orleans, or Garden of Memories or Lake Lawn Park Cemetery in Metairie, Louisiana. Friedrich's family line is then traceable through Shelby Brown another four generations, from Louisiana to Alabama and, finally, Mississippi. The apparent current end of the line is a family that has lived in coastal Mississippi for at least the last fifty years. Coincidentally, they operate a gallery dealing in pictorial art as well as glass and pottery.

10 Friedrich's drawings resemble three unsigned works attributed to Charles Herff, Ferdinand's son and previous owner of D2. Two of these works have been titled *The Hanging of Bob Augustin.* As a young boy in September 1861, Charles skipped school to watch the lynching of desperado Bob Augustine on San Antonio's

Military Plaza. Charles was disturbed by the gruesome event, and sometime later he supposedly produced two watercolored ink drawings of the spectacle. Both drawings (one in two copies) reside among Charles's papers in the Briscoe Texas History Center, University of Texas at Austin, and each has been published (Briscoe di_03433 and di_06999; di_07000; Fox 1977, 26; Steinfeldt 1981, 41; Fisher 2010, 18–19). Much of the detailing and compositional practice in both of these pictures closely resemble those in the Friedrich captive drawings; and like those drawings, these exist in a pair that contain both repetition and revision. The third work credited to Charles, an unpublished pen sketch entitled *San Antonio Scene, 1860s* and providing a wider view of the same plaza where the lynching occurred, also resembles Friedrich's drawings (Briscoe di_03434). One of the lynching pictures has been given a date of 1876–1877 (Fox 1977) and the plaza sketch is dated by the Briscoe to 1860–1870, when Charles was no more than fifteen years old. Any of these works could actually have been made by Friedrich. Otherwise, the younger Herff knew Friedrich and his drawings and must have been influenced by them. Their works in turn bear a resemblance to the four views of San Antonio's Main Plaza by Bexar County lawman and folk painter William Giles Martin Samuel (ca. 1825–1902), dated 1849 but perhaps painted later (Steinfeldt 1981, 21, 25, 28, 29; Utterback 2015). Since Herff neighbor Theodore Gentilz was also historically minded and shared Friedrich's background in drafting and surveying, he may have influenced Friedrich or Charles Herff. The concept of a nascent local style involving these men deserves further study.

CHAPTER FOUR

[1] Co-author Gelo was stuck with this nickname during his 1982 Comanche fieldwork after he decided to give up shaving. Plucked eyebrows, and a lack of facial hair among Comanches without Mexican admixture, were noted by Goldstein (1934, 291, 295). Ferdinand Herff did observe some Comanche men with "mustaches . . . allowed to grow at the corner of their mouths but . . . carefully plucked from the middle of the upper lip, [giving] them the appearance of tiger cats" (Herff 1848:43, column 677, translated by Wickham). Compare Catlin's portrait and description of Ta-wah-que-nah (Tabequena) (Catlin 1973:67 and facing).

CHAPTER SIX

[1] It has been mistakenly implied or stated that Julie Herf joined the Forty in Galveston (Herff 1973, 12–13; Morgenthaler 2007, 77). Weber, however, established that she joined shortly before their departure from Germany (Weber 1894, part 1, page 26). According to Heinemann, a "Frauenverein" (women's society) had formed in Germany to support the Forty project, and it is likely that this society, probably consisting of family members, fiancées, and brides, had a hand in selecting

Herf. She was an older woman, one we may assume was considered unlikely to compromise the morality of the group and its members. A letter from the period refers to her as a "bejahrte Dame" ("woman of advanced years") (Heinemann 1994, 300); the September 1850 New Braunfels census give her age as forty-nine. Though among the Fortiers at that point, she may have sailed over separately, as her name does not appear with those of the men on the *St. Pauli* manifest. After Bettina she remained a member of the ex-Fortier community. For a time, she cared for a group of the former settlers in New Braunfels, and she provided housekeeping at the post-Bettina commune in present Boerne (Weber 1894, part 1, page 38; part 2, page 9). The Kendall County census shows her still living there with Adam Vogt in August 1870.

2   The image of Natives serving up the bounty of nature for their visitors as an act of friendship is curiously present also in the aforementioned lithograph of Europeans meeting Hawaiians; here the Natives even carry their animal in the same way. The complicated history of pigs in Polynesia makes it uncertain whether they carry a feral or domestic hog.

CHAPTER EIGHT

1   Catfish Crossing was not at the modern Castell bridge, but one mile downstream near the original site of Castell. Here the river flows between large flat tongues of limestone forming a natural ramp in and out of the stream. Traces of the path leading across the ford are visible from FM 104 on the north side of the river. We are indebted to Glenn Hadeler for pointing out this location.

2   Assuming Friedrich was on the trip, this route also brought him directly through the property he would purchase three years later for the pre-Boerne settlement, and may well have served as his preview of the location.

3   Almost half a century later, German-American painter Albert Bierstadt chose the same perspective as Friedrich for his 1893 painting of Columbus's arrival in the New World (Wickham 1997, 106). His *The Landing of Columbus* was intended for the Chicago World's Columbian Exposition; it was rendered in multiple versions, with extant examples owned by the Newark Museum of Art and City of Plainfield, New Jersey. It depicts Columbus's party arriving triumphantly on a beach while Indians watch from the darkness of the forest in the foreground, some of them genuflecting reverently before the Europeans, offering gifts of gourds and pumpkins. The shadowy, unknown New World submits voluntarily to the light-bathed "discoverers"; the view of the Natives from the back precludes the revealing of facial expressions, but the body language is clear. Where Friedrich's

contemporaneous rendering of the arrival of the Germans conveys a hope for
comity and coexistence between the two cultures, Bierstadt's retrospective painting
imposes the interpretation of the victors four hundred years after the fact.

CHAPTER NINE

[1] There are two eyewitness accounts of the council besides those of Roemer and
the anonymous officers. Indian agent Robert Simpson Neighbors intruded upon
Meusebach's council and aided in the negotiations. His terse report is especially
disappointing in not confirming German reports of a captive offer. Neighbors
himself rescued and adopted a Mexican boy from Comanches in 1847 (Biesele 1930,
184–85; Neighbours 1975, 35-36, 100). Meusebach's own account of the council is
equally reticent, with no mention of a captive (Biesele 1930, 185–86).

CHAPTER TEN

[1] Dielmann (1954, 274) follows Weber in stating that the captive was brought
six months later. As a newer source published in English by a family member,
Peter Herff's version specifying three months (Herff 1973, 15) has proven more
influential.

[2] This name appears to be keepahmu, "no tobacco," no doubt the same person
who was among the Comanche signers of the 1850 Fort Martin Scott Treaty,
listed there as "KA-BA-HA-MO, Never Smokes" (Winfrey and Day 1995, 135;
Kavanagh 1996, 336).

[3] Coreth's estate was next to the original Darmstadt Farm. Lena's presence at Herff's
return places her at the Coreth home in January 1850 (see Herff 1848:43, column
674; Spiess Papers, 108; Dielmann 1954, 276). Augusta and Minchen were
presumably daughters of the Fortier Gustav Schleicher. In 1848 Louis Cachand
Ervendberg, Protestant minister, founded the Western Texas Orphan Asylum,
also called the Waisenhaus or Waisenfarm, in New-Wied north of New Braunfels
to care for the children of dead settlers (Geiser 1948, 113-14).

CHAPTER TWELVE

[1] The desire of the Fortiers and other upper-class German settlers to report home
and write their own history cannot be overestimated (see Heinemann 1994, 284,
identifying published and unpublished letters by several correspondents). They
were quite conscious of the polarized descriptions of the Texas settlement effort,
some painting Texas as a heaven on earth, others harshly critical of the Adelsverein
and anyone foolish enough to buy its propaganda, and they hoped to substitute their
own lived experiences. Friedrich and his young colleagues announced this intention
in the letter they published as they left Germany:

Incidentally, whatever the fate of our enterprise, which is not motivated by dire external circumstance nor by the impulse of self-interest, may be, we are as a group determined not to conceal its progress and outcome from the public, but to report the full, pure truth without any concern at all for ourselves or any third parties.

In doing this, we will not try to influence the judgement of others with glowing statements but simply allow the bare facts to speak for themselves, and we ask every right-thinking person and particularly those who know us personally to make up their own minds and not be misled by premature attacks that come partly from false information and partly from more nefarious motives, and to reserve all judgement on our undertaking until they have received definite news from us. (Friedrich, Schenck, and Schleicher 1847, column 220; trans. by Wickham).

Doubtless this compulsion was strongly encouraged by the Adelsverein commissioners, who sorely needed an antidote to the bad press their efforts constantly received; success of the Darmstadt settlement effort was critically important to the Adelsverein (see Heinemann 1994, 285–87).

2   C. D. Friedrich is celebrated for his landscapes (*The Great Enclosure near Dresden*, 1832) and seascapes (*Moonrise by the Sea*, 1822), his contemplative human figures typically placed in the foreground gazing away into the infinity of nature (*Two Men Contemplating the Moon*, 1819; *Wanderer above a Sea of Fog*, 1818), his solemnity (*Abbey in the Oak Wood*, 1810), and his heavily symbolic allegories (*The Cliffs at Rügen*, 1818; *The Stages of Life*, 1835). Apart from their backs-to-the-front and natural settings, Wilhelm Friedrich's sketches on the face of it have little in common with the paintings of Caspar David. But in a similar way to our brief discussion of Leutze, by thinking about what the painter accomplishes with his gazer-from-behind portrayals we can open a door to some of the possibilities offered by this technique and develop a clearer idea of what Wilhelm Friedrich accomplishes (and does not accomplish) with his use of it.

   According to Raffaella Russo, Caspar David Friedrich "often emphasizes the smallness of man before the infinity of nature by rendering the figures in reduced dimensions, making them symbols of the individual's deep sense of solitude and quest for a harmonious union with God" (Russo 1999, 62). While C. D. Friedrich struggles with the enormity of nature and how diminutive mankind confronts and internalizes it on a spiritual and sometimes explicitly religious level, Wilhelm Friedrich is interested in the natural environment as a context for human activity, more specifically for cross-cultural encounters. While there are weighty questions implied in these encounters, they are rooted in pragmatism and depicted as empirical experience. Where Friedrich, the Romantic painter, places emphasis on solemnity of mood and atmosphere (*Monk on the Seashore*, 1810; *On the*

Sailing Ship, 1819), the sketch artist foregrounds activity and human interaction. Contemplation, meditation and stillness characterize the one; while communication and restless movement mark the other. That said, in the work of both artists there is an inherent political dimension. C. D. Friedrich is painting at the time of the Wars of Liberation against Napoleon, and many of his images are to be read as allegorical expressions of this struggle (*The Chasseur in the Forest*, 1814). Wilhelm Friedrich's drawings contain the sociopolitical reality of competing cultures in 1840s Texas, as Comanches and Germans try to find a shared way forward but will eventually have to reckon with the inevitable. C. D. Friedrich's gazers-from-behind pose metaphysical questions that probe the nature of human existence and the interior of the self; Wilhelm Friedrich's Indians in D3, whose backs we see and whose point of view we share, challenge the viewer to see—and experience—a specific historical event with the eyes of others and, by extension, to step outside the self.

Still other prominent German artists created works which stand in instructive comparison to Friedrich's drawings. Carl Wimar (1828-1862) made two oil on canvas paintings depicting the abduction of pioneer Daniel Boone's daughter Jemima Boone by Cherokee and Shawnee Indians, an event which took place in July 1776 near Boonesboro, Kentucky. The two paintings, both entitled *The Abduction of Daniel Boone's Daughter by the Indians*, were done a few years after Friedrich's work, in 1853 and 1855-56. Wimar was a German-American from St. Louis who trained at the Düsseldorf Academy. He was very familiar with Indian neighbors from his boyhood and painted several Native subjects (see Wickham 1997, 69–72). Like Friedrich, Wimar treats the non-Indian female captive theme in his Boone paintings, though no ransom is implied in his representations. In his 1855–56 interpretation, the Indian chief in his finery stands proud, erect, and aloof, commanding the scene as three warriors pole their raft with the bound captive across a river. Where Friedrich embeds the narrative of the Mexican girl into a densely populated scene, Wimar isolates the motif of the helpless female captive of Indians to the level of a dramatically lit theatrical tableau. Friedrich emphasizes the redemption and reconciliation; Wimar stages the peril and the threat. Jemima Boone and the two Callaway girls abducted with her were rescued three days later in an attack on the kidnappers led by her father; Jemima later married one of her rescuers. She reported that the Indians treated their prisoners with kindness (Faragher 1992, 131–140; Pearl 2021). The incident was a persistent trope by the time Friedrich and Wimar produced their art, having served as inspiration for an episode in James Fenimore Cooper's *The Last of the Mohicans* (1826). There is also a hand-colored lithograph of the same event dated 1852 and attributed to Karl Bodmer (1809–1893), the Swiss-French artist who was active in Germany and who had gained fame painting Indian subjects while exploring the Missouri River with German Prince Maximilian zu Wied-Neuwied. Later images of the abduction include an illustration in William A. Crafts' *Pioneers in the Settlement of America* (Crafts 1876, 275) and Ann Rice O'Hanlon's mural in Memorial Hall at the University of Kentucky, a 1934 Works Progress Administration project.

REFERENCES

Adam-Hurst, Kathryn. 2012. "Tombstone Tuesday: Wilhelm Friedrich." In *Conrad's Stories: The Life and Times of the Conrad Adam Family in Kendall County, Texas* website, Mar. 13. Accessed June 15, 2021.

"Adressen-Verzeichnis der ehemaligen Studierenden der höheren Gewerbeschule, der technischen Schule, sowie der polytechnischen Schule, bzw. technischen Hochschule zu Darmstadt, Darmstadt 1885," Nr. 663:21.

Affidavit. 1847. Austin: Texas General Land Office, September 7.

Anderson, Val. 2019. "Every Street Tells a Story: Iron Street, Boerne, Texas. U.S.A.—Part II." *Echoes . . . from the Archives* 24 (March): 10–12. The Dietert Historical Archives, Patrick Heath Public Library, Boerne, TX.

Anon. 1847. "Texas. Expedition der deutschen Kolonisten nach der San-Saba in Texas, im Januar 1847." *Magazin für die Literatur des Auslandes* vol. 31, no. 101, 401–402; no. 102, 406–407; no. 103, 410–11; no. 104, 415-16. Edited by J. Lehmann. Berlin: von Veit.

Attocknie, Francis Joseph. 2016. *The Life of Ten Bears: Comanche Historical Narratives*. Edited by Thomas W. Kavanagh. Lincoln: University of Nebraska Press.

Audubon, John James and John Bachman. 1854. *The Viviparous Quadrupeds of North America*, vol. 3. New York V. G. Audubon.

Baird, Scott. 2010. "Texas German Gravemarkers: Lateiner, Freethinkers, and Other Intellectuals." *Journal of the German-Texas Heritage Society* 32(1):23–26.

Baker, T. Lindsay and Billy R. Harrison. 1986. *Adobe Walls: The History and Archaeology of the 1874 Trading Post.* College Station: Texas A&M University Press.

Benedict, John. 2021. "African-American History in Kendall County: The Boerne 'Flats'." *Echoes . . . from the Archives*, Spring:1–4. The Dietert Historical Archives, Patrick Heath Public Library, Boerne, TX.

Berlandier, Jean-Louis. 1969. *The Indians of Texas in 1830.* Edited by John C. Ewers and translated by Patricia Reading Leclerq. Washington, D.C.: Smithsonian Institution Press.

Biesele, Rudolph Leopold. 1930. *The History of the German Settlements in Texas, 1831–1861.* Austin: Press of Von Boeckmann-Jones. Rpt., Austin, n.p., 1964; Fort Worth: Eakin Press, 1987.

———. 1995. "German Attitudes Toward the Civil War." In *Handbook of Texas Online.* Austin: Texas State Historical Association. Accessed July 5, 2021.

Blankinship, J. W. 1907. "Plantae Lindheimerianae, Part III." In Report (Annual) of the Missouri Botanical Garden 18:123–223. St. Louis.

Boardman, Keva Hoffman. 2018. "The Friedrich Brothers, Part 1." In *Around the Sophienburg/Sophienblog* website, Nov. 25. Accessed Jan. 14, 2021.

Bracht, Viktor. 1931. *Texas in 1848.* Translated by Charles Frank Schmidt. San Antonio: Naylor. Rpt., Manchaca, TX: German-Texas Heritage Society, 1991. Orig. *Texas im Jahre 1848, Nach mehrjährigen Beobachtungen dargestellt.* Elberfeld and Iserlohn: Julius Bädeker, 1849.

Buenger, Walter L. 1979. "Secession and the Texas German Community: Editor Lindheimer vs. Editor Flake." *Southwestern Historical Quarterly* 82:379–402.

Burkhalter, Lois. 1961. *A Seth Eastman Sketchbook.* Austin: University of Texas Press.

Burnet, David G. 1851. "The Comanches and Other Tribes of Texas; and the Policy to be Pursued Respecting Them." In *Information Respecting the History, Condition and Prospects of the Indian Tribes of the United States*, vol. 1. Edited by Henry Rowe Schoolcraft, 229–41. Philadelphia: Lippincott, Grambo.

Catlin, George. 1973. *Letters and Notes on the Manners, Customs, and Conditions of North American Indians*, vol. 2. New York: Dover Publications.

Chabot, Frederick C. 1937. *With the Makers of San Antonio*. San Antonio: privately published.

Chamisso, Adelbert von. 2012. *Reise um die Welt. Mit 150 Lithographien von Ludwig Choris und einem essayistischen Nachwort von Matthias Glaubrecht*. Berlin: Die andere Bibliothek.

Clark, W. P. 1982. *The Indian Sign Language*. Lincoln: University of Nebraska Press.

Corwin, Hugh D. 1959. *Comanche and Kiowa Captives in Oklahoma and Texas*. Guthrie, OK: Cooperative Publishing Company.

Cowdrey, Mike, Ned Martin and Jody Martin. 2012. *Horses and Bridles of the American Indians*. Nicasio, CA: Hawk Hill Press.

Crafts, William A. 1876. *Pioneers in the Settlement of America: From Florida in 1510 to California in 1849*. Vol. II. Boston: Samuel Walker and Company.

DeShields, James T. 1993. *Border Wars of Texas*. Austin: State House Press. Orig., Tioga, TX: The Herald Company, 1912.

Dielmann, Henry B. 1954. "Dr. Ferdinand Herff, Pioneer Physician and Surgeon," *Southwestern Historical Quarterly* 57:265–84.

Dodge, Richard Irving. 1882. *Our Wild Indians*. Hartford, CT: A.D. Worthington.

Domenech, Emmanuel. 1858. *Missionary Adventures in Texas and Mexico*. London: Longman, Brown, Green, Longmans, and Roberts.

Dubois, Scott. 2020. "The Last Jaguar in Texas—1948." In *Wild Texas History* website. Austin: Scott Dubois. Accessed Jan. 28, 2021.

"Early Leader, Girl Kidnapped by Indians, Visitor's Forbears." 1968. *New Braunfels Herald*, Nov. 7:12C.

Engelmann, George and Asa Gray. 1845. "Plantae Lindheimerianae. An enumeration of the Plants Collected in Texas, and Distributed to Subscribers, by F. Lindheimer, with Remarks and Descriptions of New Species, &c." *Boston Journal of Natural History* 5(2): 210–64.

Evans, Brent. 2010. *Images of America: Boerne*. Charleston, SC: Arcadia Publishing.

_____. 2021. Personal communication with authors, email of January 24.

Exley, Jo Ella Powell. 2001. *Frontier Blood: The Saga of the Parker Family*. College Station: Texas A&M University Press.

Faragher, John Mack. 1992. *Daniel Boone: The Life and Legend of an American Pioneer*. New York: Holt.

Farr, Dennis. 1958. *William Etty*. London: Routledge and Kegan Paul.

Fey, Everett Anthony. 1994. *New Braunfels: The First Founders*, vol. 1. Austin: Eakin Press.

Field Notes of a Survey of 320 Acres of Land, made for Wilhelm Friedrich. 1848. Austin: Texas General Land Office, July 16.

Fisher, Lewis F. 2010. *Chili Queens, Hay Wagons and Fandangos: The Spanish Plazas in Frontier San Antonio*. San Antonio: Maverick Publishing Company.

Ford, Alice. 1998. *Edward Hicks: Painter of the Peaceable Kingdom*. Philadelphia: University of Pennsylvania Press.

Fox, Anne A. 1977. *The Archaeology and History of the Spanish Governor's Palace Park*. University of Texas at San Antonio Center for Archaeological Research, Archaeological Survey Report 31.

Friedrich, Wilhelm, Fritz Schenck, and Gustav Schleicher. 1847. "Der Texas-Verein. Erklärung." *Der deutsche Auswanderer* 14: columns 219-21. Rpt. as "Die Darmstädter Texas-Gesellschaft." *Allgemeine Auswanderungs-Zeitung* 28: column 211-12.

Geiser, Samuel Wood. 1948. *Naturalists on the Frontier*. Second edition. Dallas: Southern Methodist University.

Gelo, Daniel J., trans. and ed. 1995. *Comanche Vocabulary*. Trilingual ed. Compiled by Manuel García Rejón. Austin: University of Texas Press. Orig. 1866.

Gelo, Daniel J. and Christopher J. Wickham. 2018. *Comanches and Germans on the Texas Frontier: The Ethnology of Heinrich Berghaus*. College Station: Texas A&M University Press.

Geue, Chester William and Ethel H. Geue. 1972. *A New Land Beckoned: German Immigration to Texas, 1844–1847*. New and enl. ed. Waco: Texian Press. Orig. 1966.

Geue, Ethel H. 1970. *New Homes in a New Land: German Immigration to Texas, 1847–1861*. Waco, TX: Texian Press.

Gill, Richardson, Christopher Gill, Reeda Peel, and Javier Vasquez. 2016. "Are Elk Native to Texas? Historical and Archaeological Evidence for the Natural Occurrence of Elk in Texas." *Journal of Big Bend Studies* 28:205-70.

Goldstein, Marcus S. 1934. "Anthropometry of the Comanches." *American Journal of Physical Anthropology* 19:289–319.

Goyne, Minetta Altgelt. 1991. *A Life Among the Texas Flora: Ferdinand Lindheimer's Letters to George Engelmann*. College Station: Texas A&M University Press.

Gray, Asa. 1850. "Plantae Lindheimerianae, Part II. An Account of a Collection of Plants made by F. Lindheimer in the Western part of Texas, in the Years 1845–6, and 1847–8, with Critical Remarks, Descriptions of new Species, Etc." Boston Journal of Natural History 6(2): 141-240.

Haas, Oscar. n.d. [Manuscript note on Darmstaedter Farm]. Oscar Haas Collection, Sophienburg Museum and Archives, New Braunfels, TX. n.p.

_____. 1968. *History of New Braunfels and Comal County, Texas, 1844–1946*. Austin: Steck Company.

_____. 1972. "Congressman Gustav Schleicher Once Resident of New Braunfels." *New Braunfels Herald*, April 13: 4B, 6B.

Hämäläinen, Pekka. 2008. *The Comanche Empire*. New Haven: Yale University Press.

Heinemann, Hartmut. 1994. "'Wo der Stern im blauen Felde eine neue Welt verkündet': Die Auswanderung der Vierziger aus Darmstadt nach Texas im Jahr 1847 und ihre kommunistische Kolonie Bettina." *Archiv für hessische Geschichte und Altertumskunde*, 52: 283–352.

Herff, Ferdinand Peter. 1973. *The Doctors Herff: A Three-Generation Memoir*. 2 vols. Edited by Laura L. Barber. San Antonio: Trinity University Press.

Herff, Ferdinand von. 1848. "Bericht über die Darmstädter Communisten-Gesellschaft in Texas." *Allgemeine Auswanderungs-Zeitung*, Nr. 38–47, Sept.–Nov.

_____. 1978. *The Regulated Emigration of the German Proletariat with Special Reference to Texas, Being also a Guide for German Emigrants*. Translated by Arthur L. Fink, Jr. San Antonio: Trinity University Press. Orig. *Die geregelte Auswanderung des deutschen Proletariats mit besonderer Beziehung auf Texas, Zugleich ein Leitfaden für deutsche Auswanderer*. Frankfurt am Main: F. Varrentrapp, Ph. Krebs, 1850.

Hertzberg, H. T. and Friedrich Schenck. 1988. "A Letter from Friedrich Schenck in Texas to His Mother in Germany, 1847." *Southwestern Historical Quarterly* 92:144–65.

Hughes, Jeremiah, ed. 1846. *Niles' National Register*, vol. 70 (vol. 20, fifth series). Baltimore: Jeremiah Hughes.

Hunter, John Warren. 1924. "The Ill-Fated Schniveley Expedition." *Frontier Times* 2 (1): 12–19.

Johnson, David R. 2020. *In the Loop: A Political and Economic History of San Antonio*. San Antonio: Trinity University Press.

Jones, Lawrence T., III. 2014. *Lens on the Texas Frontier*. College Station: Texas A&M University Press.

Jordan, Gilbert J. 1976–77. "W. Steinert's View of Texas in 1849." *Southwestern Historical Quarterly* 80:57–78, 177–200, 283–301, 399–416; 81:45–72.

Jordan, Terry G. 1966. *German Seed on Texas Soil*. Austin: University of Texas Press.

Kapp, Friedrich. 1876. "Die deutsche Ansiedlung im westlichen Texas und der Mainzer Verein deutscher Fürsten, Grafen und Herren." In *Aus und über Amerika. Thatsachen und Erlebnisse*, vol. 1, 243–90. Berlin: Julius Springer. Orig. 1855.

Kavanagh, Thomas W. 1996. *Comanche Political History*. Lincoln: University of Nebraska Press.

Kearney, James C. 2010. *Nassau Plantation: The Evolution of a Texas German Slave Plantation*. Denton: University of North Texas Press.

Kendall, Dorothy Steinbomer and Carmen Perry. 1974. *Gentilz: Artist of the Old Southwest*. Austin: University of Texas Press.

Kendall, George Wilkins. 2004. *Narrative of the Texas Santa Fé Expedition*, vol 1. Dallas: Southern Methodist University.

King, Irene Marschall. 1967. *John O. Meusebach: German Colonizer in Texas*. Austin: University of Texas Press.

Labadie, Joe, Kathy Labadie, Terry Sayther, and Deborah Stuart. 1997. "A First Look at the El Caido Site: A Historic Rock Art Site in Far Northern Coahuila, Mexico." *La Tierra* 24:14–31.

Land Grant Files. Austin: Texas General Land Office.

Laubin, Reginald and Gladys Laubin. 1980. *American Indian Archery*. Norman: University of Oklahoma Press.

Lauckhard, Fritz. 1931. "Auswandererbriefe aus Texas 1848/49." *Volk und Scholle* 9:95–101.

Lich, Glen E. 1996. *The German Texans*. San Antonio: Institute of Texan Cultures.

Lindheimer, Ferdinand. 1848. "Colonie der Darmstädter Communisten-Gesellschaft." *Allgemeine Auswanderungs-Zeitung*, Nr. 49, Dec.

_____. 1879. *Aufsätze und Abhandlungen von Ferdinand Lindheimer in Texas*. Herausgegeben von einem seiner Schüler [Gustav Passavant, ed.]. Frankfurt a.M.: Theodor Wentz. See also Williams 2020.

Lorbiecki, Marybeth. 2000. *Painting the Dakota: Seth Eastman at Fort Snelling*. St. Paul, MN: Ramsey County Historical Society.

Lowry, Shannon. 2019. "Hill Country Brothers Create Magnificent Murals." *Rock and Vine*, fall.

Mails, Thomas E. 1995. *The Mystic Warriors of the Plains*. New York: Marlowe and Company.

Marcy, Randolph B. 1866. *Thirty Years of Army Life on the Border*. New York: Harper & Brothers.

Martin, Ned, Jody Martin, and Robert Bauver. 2010. *Bridles of the Americas, Vol. 1: Indian Silver*. Nicasio, CA: Hawk Hill Press.

McDermott, John Francis. 1961. *Seth Eastman: Pictorial Historian of the Indian*. Norman: University of Oklahoma Press.

McGuire, James Patrick. 1976. *Iwonski in Texas: Painter and Citizen*. San Antonio: San Antonio Museum Association.

_____. 1983. *Hermann Lungkwitz*. Austin: University of Texas Press.

Moon, Bryden. 2020. "Two Ancient Kendall County Trails, Part 4." *Echoes . . . from the Archives* Spring:7–9. The Dietert Historical Archives, Patrick Heath Public Library, Boerne, TX.

Morgenthaler, Jefferson. 2007. *The German Settlement of the Texas Hill Country*. Boerne, TX: Mockingbird Books.

_____. 2014. *Boerne: A Brief History*. Boerne, TX: Mockingbird Books. Orig. *Boerne, Settlement on the Cibolo*, 2005.

"Namensverzeichniß der Darmstädter Texasauswanderer." 1847. *Der deutsche Auswanderer. Centralblatt der deutschen Auswanderung und Colonisirung*. Redaktion: F. Haas, Dr. Künzel in Darmstadt und Dr. H. Malten in Mainz. C.W. Leske Buchhandlung in Darmstadt. 15: columns 239-40.

Neff, Emily Ballew. 2000. *Frederic Remington: The Hogg Brothers Collection of the Museum of Fine Arts, Houston*. Princeton, NJ: Princeton University Press.

Neighbours, Kenneth Franklin. 1975. *Robert Simpson Neighbors and the Texas Frontier, 1836-1859*. Waco, TX: Texian Press.

Newcomb, William W. and Mary S. Carnahan. 1978. *German Artist on the Texas Frontier: Friedrich Richard Petri*. Austin: University of Texas Press.

Noyes, Stanley. 1999. *Comanches in the New West, 1895-1908*. Austin: University of Texas Press.

Parker, William B. 1856. *Notes Taken during the Expedition Commanded by Capt. R. B. Marcy, U.S.A., through Unexplored Texas, in the Summer and Fall of 1854*. Philadelphia: Hayes and Zell.

Pearl, Matthew. 2021. *The Taking of Jemima Boone*. New York: Harper.

Penniger, Robert. 1896. *Fest-Ausgabe zum fünfzigjährigen Jubiläum der Deutschen Kolonie Friedrichsburg*. Fredericksburg, TX: Robert Penniger.

_____. 1971. *Fredericksburg, Texas: The First Fifty Years*. Translated by Dr. Charles L. Wisseman Sr. Fredericksburg, TX: Fredericksburg Publishing. Translation of Penniger 1896.

_____. 2020. *Fredericksburg, Texas: The First Fifty Years*. Fredericksburg, TX: Gillespie County Historical Society. Rpt. of Penniger 1971.

Petition for a New County. 1855. Manuscript, Texas State Archives, Austin.

Petition for a New County. 1859. Manuscript, Texas State Archives, Austin.

Phelps, Robert. 2021. Personal communication to authors, email of January 24.

Ragsdale, Crystal Sasse. 2010. "Spiess, Lena." in *Handbook of Texas Online*. Austin: Texas State Historical Association. Accessed February 3, 2021.

Ratcliffe, Sam D. 1991. "*Escenas de Martirio*: Notes on *The Destruction of the Mission San Sabá*." *Southwestern Historical Quarterly* 94: 507–34.

Reichstein, Andreas V. 2001. *German Pioneers on the American Frontier: The Wagners of Texas and Illinois*. Denton: University of North Texas Press.

Reinhardt, Louis. 1899. "The Communistic Colony of Bettina (1846-48)." *Quarterly of the Texas State Historical Association* 3(1):33–40. Based on interview with Rudolph Kleberg, Jr. Also published as "Texas Communistic Colony" in *Houston Daily Post*, Sunday, August 13, 1899.

Rhoads, Alice J. 2010. "Mason County." In *Handbook of Texas Online*. Austin: Texas State Historical Association. Accessed January 20, 2021.

Richardson, Rupert Norval. 1996. *The Comanche Barrier to South Plains Settlement.* Austin: Eakin Press. Orig. 1933, Glendale, CA: Arthur H. Clark Company.

Rivaya-Martínez, Joaquín. 2006. "Captivity and Adoption among the Comanche Indians." Unpublished PhD diss. University of California—Los Angeles, Department of Anthropology.

Robinson, Michael J. 2006. "Suitable Habitat for Jaguars in New Mexico." Report to the Habitat Subcommittee of the Jaguar Conservation Team. Tucson, AZ: Center for Biological Diversity.

Roe, Frank Gilbert. 1955. *The Indian and the Horse.* Norman: University of Oklahoma Press.

Roemer, Ferdinand von. 1849. *Texas. Mit besonderer Rücksicht auf deutsche Auswanderung.* Bonn: Adolph Marens.

_____. 1983. *Texas, with Particular Reference to the German Immigration and the Physical Appearance of the Country.* Translated by Oswald Mueller. San Marcos, TX: German-Texas Heritage Society. Orig. San Antonio: Standard Printing, 1935. Translation of Roemer 1849.

Russo, Raffaella. 1999. *Friedrich. German Master of the Romantic Landscape—His Life in Paintings.* Trans. by Anna Bennett. New York: D. K. Publishing.

Scharfenberg, Karl and Wilhelm Fabricius. 1890. *Geschichte des Corps Starkenburgia zu Gießen von 1840-1890. Zur Erinnerung an den Fünfzigjährigen Stiftungscommers zu Gießen am 7., 8. u. 9. August 1890.* Berlin: G. Schuh.

Schmied, Wieland. 1975. *Caspar David Friedrich.* Köln: Dumont Schauberg.

Shapiro, Michael Edward and Peter H. Hassrick. 1991. *Frederic Remington: The Masterworks.* New York: Harry N. Abrams, Inc. in association with The St. Louis Art Museum. Orig. 1988.

Smithwick, Noah. 1983. *The Evolution of a State, or Recollections of Old Texas Days.* Austin: University of Texas Press.

Sörgel, Alwin H. 1992. *A Sojourn in Texas, 1846-47: Alwin H. Sörgel's Texas Writings.* Translated and edited by W. M. Von-Maszewski. San Marcos: German-Texan Heritage Society, Southwest Texas State University.

Spiess Papers. Typescript of notes and letters by Hermann Spiess and associates. Compiled by Clyde H. Porter, translated by Oswald Mueller, circa 1950. Vertical files, Institute of Texan Cultures, University of Texas at San Antonio.

Steinert, Wilhelm. 1850. *Nordamerika, vorzüglich Texas im Jahre 1849.* Berlin: K. W. Kruger's Verlagshandlung.

Steinfeldt, Cecilia. 1981. *Texas Folk Art: One Hundred Fifty Years of the Southwestern Tradition.* Austin: Texas Monthly Press.

Tiling, Moritz. 1913. *History of the German Element in Texas from 1820-1850.* Houston: Moritz Tiling.

ULB. Universitäts- und Landesbibliothek Darmstadt. Digitale Sammlungen. UA Darmstadt Bestand 100: Hochschulverwaltung vor 1945: Matrikel- und Zensurbücher (Zensurbuch der Höheren Gewerbeschule 1836–1841).

ULB. Universitäts- und Landesbibliothek Darmstadt. Digitale Sammlungen. UA Darmstadt Bestand 100: Hochschulverwaltung vor 1945: Matrikel- und Zensurbücher (Zensurbuch der oberen Abteilungen 1841–1843).

Utterback, Martha. 2015. "Samuel, William Giles Martin," In *Handbook of Texas Online.* Austin: Texas State Historical Association. Accessed June 1, 2021.

Viola, Herman J. 1995. *Diplomats in Buckskins: A History of Indian Delegations in Washington City.* Bluffton, SC: Rivolo Books.

Wallace, Ernest and E. Adamson Hoebel. 1952. *The Comanches: Lords of the South Plains.* Norman: University of Oklahoma Press.

Weber, Adolf Paul, ed. 1894. *Deutsche Pioniere: zur Geschichte des Deutschtums in Texas.* 2 parts in 1 volume. San Antonio: Selbstverlag des Verfassers.

Weniger, Del. 1997. *The Explorers' Texas: Vol. 2, The Animals They Found.* Austin: Eakin Press.

Wickham, Christopher J. 1997. "Oil and Water: The Development of the Portrayal of Native Americans by Nineteenth-Century German Painters." *Yearbook of German-American Studies* 31: 63-106.

Wilbarger, J. W. 1985. *Indian Depredations in Texas.* Austin: Eakin Press. Orig. Austin: Hutchings, 1889.

Williams, John E. 2020. *The Writings of Ferdinand Lindheimer: Texas Botanist, Texas Philosopher.* College Station: Texas A&M University Press. Translation of Lindheimer 1879.

Winfrey, Dorman H. and James M. Day. 1995. *The Indian Papers of Texas and the Southwest, 1825-1916.* Vol. 3. Austin: Texas State Historical Association. Orig. 1966.

Wurster, Ilse. 2008. *Die Kettner Briefe. Kettner Letters: A Firsthand Account of a German Immigrant in the Texas Hill Country (1850-1875).* Edited by Charles Kettner. Translated by Peter Benje, Carol Okeson, and Jerry Okeson. Wilmington, DE: Comanche Creek Press.

Zesch, Scott. 2004. *The Captured.* New York: St. Martin's Press.

INDEX

CPSIA information can be obtained
at www.ICGtesting.com
Printed in the USA
JSHW040912261122
33604JS00006B/17